CHEKHOV

in an hour

CAROL ROCAMORA

SUSAN C. MOORE, SERIES

T0204356

PLAYWRIGHTS in an hour
know the playwright, love the play

IN AN HOUR BOOKS • HANOVER, NEW HAMPSHIRE • INANHOURBOOKS.COM
AN IMPRINT OF SMITH AND KRAUS PUBLISHERS, INC • SMITHANDKRAUS.COM

With grateful thanks to Carl R. Mueller,
whose fascinating introductions to his translations of the Greek and
German playwrights provided inspiration for this series.

Published by In an Hour Books
an imprint of Smith and Kraus, Inc.
177 Lyme Road, Hanover, NH 03755
inanhourbooks.com SmithandKraus.com

Know the playwright, love the play.

In an Hour, In a Minute, and Theater IQ are registered trademarks of
In an Hour Books.

Front cover design by Dan Mehling, dmehling@gmail.com
Text design by Kate Mueller, Electric Dragon Productions
Book production by Dede Cummings Design, DCDesign@sover.net

ISBN-13: 978-1-936232-00-0
ISBN-10: 1-936232-00-6
Library of Congress Control Number: 2009943211

CONTENTS

Why Playwrights in an Hour?

This new series by Smith and Kraus Publishers titled Playwrights in an Hour has a dual purpose for being; one academic, the other general. For the general reader, this volume, as well as the many others in the series, offers in compact form the information needed for a basic understanding and appreciation of the works of each volume's featured playwright. Which is not to say that there don't exist volumes on end devoted to each playwright under consideration. But inasmuch as few are blessed with enough time to read the splendid scholarship that is available, a brief, highly focused accounting of the playwright's life and work is in order.

The central feature of the series, a thirty- to forty-page essay, integrates the playwright into the context of his or her time and place. And the volumes, though written to high standards of academic integrity, are accessible in style and approach to the general reader as well as to the student, and of course to the theater professional and theatergoer.

These books will serve for the brushing up of one's knowledge of a playwright's career, to the benefit of theater work or theatergoing. The Playwrights in an Hour series represents all periods of Western theater: Aeschylus to Shakespeare to Wedekind to Ibsen to Williams to Beckett, and on to the great contemporary playwrights who continue to offer joy and enlightenment to a grateful world.

Carl R. Mueller
School of Theater, Film and Television
Department of Theater
University of California, Los Angeles

Introduction

Anton Chekhov is arguably the greatest playwright of the modern period. Yet, his reputation rests on a handful of plays — only four have permanently entered the repertory. Each of these works, moreover, is written in an unmistakable signature style. Unlike August Strindberg or Bertolt Brecht, Chekhov refrains from showy experimentation; and, unlike Henrik Ibsen, he is content with exploring a single social theme.

That theme is the radical change in Russian society that led to the revolutions of 1905 and 1917. About these changes, Chekhov takes no single political view. There are few playwrights who are more aloof, more distant from the opinions of their characters, who are more deeply involved with what they do than what they say. Yet, despite this appearance of detachment, no other playwright is as deeply invested in the future of the human race or more regretful about the prostration of the cultured elite before the forces of provincial darkness than Chekhov. Chekhov's writing is full of paradoxes — at once comic and tragic, engaged and impartial, subjective and objective. He creates no heroes or author's surrogates; yet, we are never in doubt about the value he puts on human life.

Chekhov's four major plays sometimes seem to be one long play, focusing on the same class of aristocratic characters curdling in the country, engaged in the same debates about culture and provincialism, concluding with the same sense of ambiguous possibility, torn between hope and despair. *The Seagull* is unashamedly a play about literature and love, featuring two sets of actors, two writers, two views of the stage (realistic and visionary), and three love triangles. That the one of these has an incestuous component underlines the play's parallels with Shakespeare's *Hamlet*.

Like *The Seagull, Uncle Vanya* is a play about hope and disillusionment. Vanya has lost all respect for his one-time idol, the academician Serebreyakov, and he is in love with the professor's bored wife, Yelena. So in a more desultory way is Doctor Astrov. But Yelena is too indolent to be unfaithful. Eventually, Vanya's loss of faith in the future produces despair. By the end of the play Vanya has come very close to the suicide that ended the life of Constantine Treplev.

Three Sisters, one of Chekhov's two indisputable masterpieces, is also about the loss of a comforting ideal. The Prozorov sisters have spent most of their mature lives in a provincial military town, longing to return to Moscow. Masha is unhappily married to a schoolteacher; Irina is about to wed a soldier she admires but does not love; Olga is stuck in a boring job as a schoolteacher. Meanwhile, their sister-in-law, Natasha is eating away at their ancestral home like a carpenter ant, moving the sisters from one room to another and eventually out of the house in order to accommodate her crude maternal, social, and adulterous needs. *Three Sisters* is the bleakest play Chekhov ever wrote.

Composed with great difficulty while he was dying, *The Cherry Orchard* is, nevertheless, the most comical of his full-length plays, and it may be his greatest work of art. In the tradition of a French mortgage melodrama — plays about villainous overseers stealing the property of impoverished aristocrats — the play focuses on the loss of an ancestral estate whose aristocratic owners are too distracted to save it. In the speeches of the perpetual graduate student, Trofimov, we hear condemnations of the serf system and rumbles of the coming revolution; yet, he too is so paralyzed he can do nothing about it but speechify. Ultimately the estate falls into the hands of the bourgeois Lopakhin, who, far from being a villainous overseer, is the hardest-working man in the area.

Chekhov sketches out a grand panorama of history through the lives of a few idle aristocrats. Through characters like Lopakhin, the descendent of a serf, Chekhov leaves us in no doubt where his political sympathies lie. But as an artist who is humane to the marrow of his bones, he embraces virtually every one of his characters with deep-felt sympathy. Standing on the threshold of the modern world, Chekhov prophesies a future in which, as Yeats said, the best lack conviction, and the worst are full of passionate intensity.

Robert Brustein
Founding Director of the Yale and American Repertory Theatres
Distinguishing Scholar in Residence, Suffolk University

Chekhov

IN A MINUTE

A snapshot of the playwright's world. From historical events to culture and the literary landscape of the time, this brief list catalogues events that directly or indirectly had an impact on the playwright's writing. Play citations refer to premiere dates.

Chekhov

DRAMATIC WORKS

Platonov
On the High Road
On the Harmful Effects of Tobacco
Ivanov
Swan Song
The Bear
The Proposal
Tatyana Repina
A Tragedian in Spite of Himself
The Wedding
The Wood Demon
The Jubilee
The Night before the Trial
The Seagull
Uncle Vanya
The Three Sisters
The Cherry Orchard

NARRATIVE FICTION

Chekhov's narrative fiction comprises some 588 short stories.

This section presents a complete list of the playwright's works in chronological order.

ONSTAGE WITH CHEKHOV

Introducing Colleagues and Contemporaries of Chekhov

THEATER

Bertolt Brecht, German playwright and poet
Maxim Gorky, Russian novelist and playwright
Henrik Ibsen, Norwegian playwright
Konstantin Stanislavsky, Russian director
August Strindberg, Swedish playwright
Lev Tolstoy, Russian novelist
Ivan Turgenev, playwright, novelist, short story writer
Oscar Wilde, Irish playwright

ARTS

Edvard Munch, Norwegian painter
Sergey Rachmaninov, Russian composer, pianist, and conductor
Auguste Rodin, French sculptor
Alexsandr Scriabin, Russian composer
Pyotr Tchaikovsky, Russian composer
Vincent Van Gogh, Dutch painter
Giuseppe Verdi, Italian composer
Richard Wagner, German composer

This section lists contemporaries whom the playwright may or may not have known.

POLITICS/MILITARY

Otto Von Bismarck, German statesman

Benjamin Disraeli, British prime minister

Alfred Dreyfus, French army officer

Ferdinand I, king of Bulgaria

Vladimir Lenin, Russian revolutionary, Bolshevik communist

Nicholas II, last Russian czar

Oswald Spengler, German historian

Queen Victoria, British monarch

PHILOSOPHY/RELIGION

Henri Bergson, French philosopher

G. K. Chesterton, English Christian apologist

Johann Wilhelm Herrmann, German theologian

Theodor Herzl, founder of Jewish Zionism

Karl Marx, German philosopher, political economist

Friedrich Nietzsche, German philosopher

Charles Peirce, American logician

Herbert Spencer, English philosopher

LITERATURE

Matthew Arnold, English poet and essayist

Joseph Conrad, Polish-born English novelist

Fyodor Dostoevsky, Russian novelist

Guy de Maupassant, French writer

Herman Melville, American writer

Rainer Maria Rilke, Austrian poet

Paul Verlaine, French poet

Emile Zola, French novelist

SCIENCE

Niels Bohr, Danish physicist
Charles Darwin, English naturalist
Thomas Edison, American inventor
Albert Einstein, German-born physicist
Sigmund Freud, Austrian psychologist
Richard von Krafft-Ebing, German neurologist
Carl Jung, Swiss psychologist
Max Planck, German physicist

INDUSTRY/BUSINESS

Alexander Graham Bell, American inventor of telephone
Karl Benz, German engineer; inventor of first four-wheel car
Henry Ford, American automaker
King C. Gillette, American inventor of safety razor
Alfred Krupp, German industrialist
Alfred Nobel, Swedish inventor of dynamite
Cecil Rhodes, English mining magnate
John D. Rockefeller, American oil baron

SPORTS

Meriwether Lewis Clark Jr., founder of Kentucky Derby
"Gentleman Jim" Corbett, American boxing champion
Pierre de Coubertin, organizer of modern Olympic games
W. G. Grace, English cricketer
William Muldoon, American wrestler
Lady Margaret Scott, English golf champion
John L. Sullivan, the first great American boxing champion
May G. Sutton, English tennis champion

CHEKHOV

in an hour

RUSSIA BEFORE CHEKHOV

Nineteenth-century Imperial Russia, where Anton Pavlovich Chekhov lived and wrote, was a land larger than the entire American continent. It covered eight-and-one-half million square miles, or one-sixth of the world's inhabitable surface. Nowhere at the time was there a continuous stretch of territory in the world, ruled by a single ruler, of comparable size to the Russian Empire. Stretching from Eastern Europe all the way across Siberia to the Pacific Coast, the land was vast, varied, and dramatically diverse in terrain. Indeed, with its immense forests, great rivers, wide steppes, towering mountain ranges, and extreme climate (ranging from Arctic to subtropic), it seemed like another planet. Divided by the Ural Mountain range, the country was, like the Greek god, "Janus-faced." Russia west of the Urals looked to Europe for its cultural model, while the Russia east of the Urals was called "Asiatic." At the time, this meant backward, desolate, and impenetrable. When Chekhov himself journeyed across the entire country in 1890 by a combination of train and cart, it took him months. At the turn of the

---

This is the core of the book. The essay places the playwright in the context of his or her world and analyzes the influences and inspirations within that world.

century, the railroad was finally completed. It still took a week to cross the country by train.

This vast empire was under the rigid, autocratic rule of the Romanov family. They had ruled since the 1600s. Comprising the royalty was first and foremost the czar and his family. There was also a handful of titled aristocracy, including princes, counts, and barons. The czar's system of governance was archaic and clumsy. It had been established in 1722 by Peter the Great. It consisted of a pretentious hierarchy of fourteen official ranks (i.e., a civil service), which remained in place until 1917. Members of the hierarchy had cumbrous titles, ornate uniforms, and elaborate decorations. This gave writers of the nineteenth century rich material for satire — when they could get past the censor. The function of the civil service — indeed of all governmental organs, including the Ministry and the Senate — was to implement the czar's will, rather than to set policy. In Chekhov's time, Czar Aleksandr II (1855–81) made an attempt at reform of the local government system with the establishment of town and rural councils. However, the czarist government kept close watch on these local councils, lest they exercise any kind of political autonomy.

THE CLASSES

The monolithic social structure of the country was divided into classifications or "estates." The clergy was just under 1 percent of the total population. The landed gentry was considered a suborder of the nobility without title and it was just over 1 percent of the population. The military made up 6.5 percent of the population, and the town dwellers equaled 9 percent, including merchants. This was the class to which Chekhov's family belonged. Doctors, lawyers, architects, teachers, and other professionals came from several of the above groups. The remaining and vast majority of the population consisted of the peasantry, or former serfs, and represented 81.5 percent of the population. They lived in medieval conditions of poverty and squalor. They were subject to the extremes of the climate, famine, and disease. On the other hand, the landed gentry lived in a world of its own, speaking primarily French and other Western languages. They were often unable to read or write in Russian. Both the gentry and the clergy were exempt from taxation, conscription, and corporal punishment. As the owners of "souls," the gentry had complete control over the lives of their serfs. They could buy them and sell them, subject them to corporal punishment, and enlist them in the Russian army at their whim.

During Chekhov's lifetime, the population grew at a rapid rate, from roughly 74 million in 1860 to over 133 million by 1904. It was a large, complex population, representing 200 different nationalities, speaking dozens of languages.

As for its economy, Chekhov's times saw the beginnings of rapid industrialization in Russia in an effort to keep up with its European neighbors, behind whom it lagged significantly. As a result, there were severe social consequences, and the working and living conditions of the workers (drawn from the former serfs) were dire. The gap between the new industrial working class and the czarist regime widened even more sharply. This created fertile soil for extremism, foment, and disorder.

In short, nineteenth-century Imperial Russia was a huge, backward empire. It was unwieldy in size and unjust in governance. Political, social, and economic changes were desperately long overdue. That is what makes the study of Chekhov's life and work so interesting. In his plays and short stories, one sees a huge country and a great culture in flux. It is moving toward the final stages of what would be a tremendous and dramatic transformation. Chekhov's plays themselves are harbingers of these changes.

REVOLUTION IN THE AIR

This was the Russia into which Anton Pavlovich Chekhov was born. His lifetime spanned an extraordinary period in Russia's history, one of enormous political and social change. He was born in 1860 — one year before the greatest social upheaval in that land in centuries. In the next year, the emancipation of the serfs representing the vast majority of the population occurred. He died in 1904. This was one year before the first of what would be two definitive revolutions. These would over-throw the centuries-old, rigid, autocratic rule of the Romanov family, and they would catapult that giant land into the modern era. In that brief period alone, Chekhov would observe — and write about — these huge changes. They included the vast shifting of the population off the estates and into the cities. This deepened the poverty and mis-ery of the lower classes. Chekhov also saw the rise of industrialization, and the emergence of a capitalistic middle class. He witnessed the weakening of the Orthodox Church, the corrosion of czarist rule, the decline of the landed gentry, and the decay of the ineffectual intelli-gentsia. It was replaced by a new political vanguard with revolutionary ideas. Again, references to all these elements can be found in his four major plays, each of which captures a moment in time — what came before, and what would come after.

RUSSIA MEETS THE WEST

As a result of Napoleon's invasion of Moscow in 1812, the Russian Army occupied Paris. This occupation opened the eyes of Russians to the huge changes in the West. It also underlined the woeful gap in Russia's own cultural and economic development. Russian soldiers — gentry and serfs alike — returned to Moscow and began to question the backward ways of their country. After the death of Czar Aleksandr I in December 1825, a group of young noblemen began to call for an enlightened new czar. They hoped he would lead their backward country into a new period of modernization and political reform. They wanted a constitution, reli-gious tolerance, and increased freedom of expression. Called the Decem-brists (named after the month in which they submitted their proposals), they were met by the severest opposition from the new Czar Nicholas I.

He was terrified by their demands and ordered the execution of their leaders and the exile of their followers.

Meanwhile, a passionate young intelligentsia was galvanizing. They were inspired by the idealistic example of the thwarted Decembrists. They included the anarchist Michael Bakunin, the critic Vissarion Belinsky, the philosopher Nicholas Stankevich, and the writer Alexander Herzen. The poet Nicolas Ogarev and the novelist Ivan Turgenev also joined them. All these men, with the exception of Belinsky, were of the nobility. Ignited by philosophy and political thought from Germany and France, they congregated in Moscow University circles. They spoke of their hopes and dreams for changing Russia. While they met and talked and dreamed, their intellectual circles widened and their ideas spread. Meanwhile, Czar Nicholas's severely reactionary regime instituted even harsher restrictions on freedom of speech, thought, and artistic creativity. Philosophy could not be taught in the universities. Censorship was absolute, the czar's secret police were everywhere, and the young intelligentsia was persecuted. Herzen was eventually banished and stripped of his noble rank. Stankevich and Belinsky died young from tuberculosis. Still their ideas spread, and the exiled Herzen would mobilize an émigré community and continue to proselytize for change.

A DECADE OF GREAT REFORMS

The advent of Czar Aleksandr II to the throne in 1855, five years before Chekhov's birth, ushered in a decade of great reforms. This led to the freeing of the serfs in 1861, only one year after Chekhov was born. Other reforms included the introduction of trials by jury and a new local government system — the *zemstvos*. There were improvements in health care and local school reforms. Despite these attempts, there continued to be no freedom of the press or open criticism of government. So social critics of the 1860s found that they could get around the censors by writing about art and literature. Thus, artistic and literary criticism became a venue for the expression of political ideas.

Czar Aleksandr II was assassinated in 1881, when Chekhov was twenty-one. This ushered in a new era of extreme reaction and police rule under his successor, Aleksandr III (1881–94). Still, Russia had begun its period of rapid economic development. The landed gentry weakened, and bankers and industrialists rose to take their place. The bureaucracy and the army remained the society's mainstay. With the advent of Nicholas II (1894–1917), industrialization was fully underway.

Meanwhile, the seeds of revolution had been sown. In the 1840s and 1850s, intellectuals were divided into two camps. The Westerniz-ers, like Herzen, looked to Europe as a model of enlightenment and progress for Russia. The Slavophils, like Dostoevsky, turned their backs on Europe and looked eastward to the true, profound Russia. By the 1860s, when Chekhov was born, radicals emerged like Chernyshevsky, who preached nihilism. The year 1870 was pivotal, as Herzen died and Lenin was born. In the 1880s, Marxism infiltrated Russia. By the end of the decade, *Das Kapital* was the most widely read book among Russian students. The Social Democrat movement emerged. Proponents were Marxist in thinking, and they looked to the working classes to promote change. At the same time, the Populist movement looked to the peasants, hoping to foment violence to create disorder. In the early 1900s, the Bolsheviks emerged with Lenin as a leading voice. His "What Is to Be Done" appeared in 1902. By 1905, the year after Chekhov's death, a number of elements combined to create a time ripe for uprising. These included strikes and disturbances in both town and country. Revolutionary groups worked to stir up peasants and workers. To this was added the humiliating defeat in the Sino-Japanese War. A demonstration in St. Petersburg on January 22, 1905 (Bloody Sunday), resulted in soldiers opening fire on the crowd. This brought on the first Russian Revolution.

Chekhov's play of 1900, *The Three Sisters*, was written only four years before his death. In this play, two characters, Tusenbach and

Vershinin, dream of what life will be like in 200 to 300 years. If only Chekhov had lived fifteen or twenty years longer, one can imagine his amazement at the acceleration of the changes he predicted in his plays. These changes would culminate in the greatest upheaval of his country's history. They brought the destruction of an autocratic order centuries old, the entire upheaval of a mammoth society, and the advent of the great Bolshevik Revolution.

THE RUSSIAN THEATER IN CHEKHOV'S TIME

In a letter to Leontyev dated November 7, 1888, Chekhov wrote about theater. He said, "The contemporary theater is like a rash, a bad urban disease. It is necessary to sweep away this disease with a broom . . . "

Unlike the grand English and French theater traditions that had produced playwrights like Shakespeare and Molière, the Russian theater into which Chekhov was born had not yet had a golden age. At the beginning of the nineteenth century, the Russian theater was controlled by the czar, as was every other aspect of life. The Heritage Court Theater in the Winter Palace, the Imperial Theaters (the Bolshoi in Moscow — used mostly for opera and ballet — and the Maly and later Aleksandrinsky in St. Petersburg) dominated the theater scene. All other popular theaters were controlled by the state as "noncourt" theaters. In addition, there was a network of provincial theaters.

With the advent of Czar Nicolas I and his repressive rule in 1825 came a harsh decree placing all public theatrical performances under the Imperial Theaters in St. Petersburg and Moscow. Then, in 1847, the existing censorship law was expanded to control all theaters, both urban and provincial. Because of these harsh controls, the marginal theaters were the only source of creativity and freedom in the Russian theater. These were the fairgrounds, street shows, cabarets, amateur drawing-room theatricals, and salons that were less closely watched by the secret police.

CENSORSHIP AND THE RUSSIAN THEATER

Despite government censorship, four major Russian plays were written in the nineteenth century before Chekhov came on the scene. The first, Griboyedov's *Wit Works Woe* (1824), was a satire on Moscow society. It initially met with censorship. It was finally premiered in 1831, two years after the playwright's death. Its protagonist, Chatsky, an angry young man who speaks his mind, became the model for the young Russian romantic hero. The second — *Boris Godunov* (1824), written by Russia's revered poet Pushkin in episodic style — was published in 1830. (Though it has been staged subsequently, it was most successful as the libretto for Mussorgsky's opera.) The third play, Gogol's *Inspector General* (1836), was a widely popular farce about corruption and ineptitude in the Russian provincial government. It became a favorite of Czar Nicholas I. The fourth, Turgenev's *A Month in the Country* (1855), was considered to be the first play of "psychological realism." It would be the one that would most influence Chekhov a half century later.

Four isolated plays by four different playwrights were scarcely enough to form the foundation of a dramatic literature or a national repertoire. It was hardly a precedent for an emerging playwright and his place in the Russian theater. By the mid-nineteenth century, there was still no treasure trove of Russian dramatic literature. In the 1840s at the Maly Theater, for example, Schiller, Molière, Goldoni, French vaudevilles, and melodramas dominated the repertoire. Then, in the 1850s, the playwright Aleksandr Ostrovsky emerged and dominated the theater scene. His extensive oeuvre included forty-seven plays about the Russian merchant class and the rural gentry. They were staged at the Maly until his death in 1886. The first to champion the right of playwrights to receive royalties, he fought in vain to found a national theater based on a Russian repertoire.

CENSORSHIP AND THE CRITICS

Not only did the government served as censor, but as critic as well — although in an unofficial capacity. A literary work, according to the government, must be topical, relevant, and socially critical. Furthermore, it must have some meaningful social content. With this view, critics looked to art and literature for a high standard of social relevance. They imposed a rigid system of criteria, both in form and content, to which all literature must conform. Critics of the 1860s, '70s, and '80s, for example, lobbied against fantasy, imagination, poetry, mysticism, and physiological perception in the theater. All literature and theater, they believed, was required to be didactic and contain some obvious social relevance. This became the norm in Chekhov's time. He would fight against this utilitarian approach valiantly, advocating personal freedom for writers and for literature. In turn, he would meet with great opposition from the critics. They felt that his humorous stories were fine, but not his serious ones. They perceived these as subversive, an affront to Russian realism in the tradition of Turgenev and Gogol. Indeed, one critic, Nikolai Mikhailovsky, the leading critic of the day, systematically tried to discredit Chekhov. His ultimate failure most likely led to the eventual liberation of Russian literature from this utilitarian standard.

Given this tradition of Russian criticism, it is no surprise that the critics of Chekhov's time could not understand his plays. Few appreciated the newness of his views and the originality of his forms. They came around long after, when his work was exported to England and America by the touring Moscow Art Theatre. Then world criticism began to appreciate Chekhov's profound contribution to modern drama. Instead, admiration and recognition for Chekhov came from his contemporaries. Notably his fellow writers Tolstoy, Gorky, Bunin, and Kuprin extolled the beauty of his craft. They appreciated the uniqueness of his vision and the depth of his humanity.

CHEKHOV: THE LIFE

In a letter dated October 11, 1899, Chekhov wrote the following: "Autobiography? I have a disease — autobiographophobia. To read any sort of details about myself, or worse, to write them for publication, is true torture for me."

Given the brevity of his lifetime (1860–1904), the accomplishments of the Russian writer Anton Pavlovich Chekhov — grandson of a serf and son of a shopkeeper — are nothing short of remarkable. In his forty-four short years, Chekhov played many roles. He was a doctor, humorist, humanist, landowner, environmentalist, social activist, and provider for a large family. At the same time, he was struggling with consumption, the first signs of which appeared when he was twenty-four. Even so, he managed to produce a veritable outpouring of prose writings that fill thirty volumes of his complete collected works. These include 588 short stories and over 4,000 letters to friends, family, writers, artists, and thinkers of his day.

Chekhov also wrote plays: eleven short works and seven full-lengths. This was a far more modest output compared with his prose work. Yet, their impact on the world stage has been enormous. This is particularly true of the final four, which are called "the major plays" — *The Seagull, Uncle Vanya, The Three Sisters,* and *The Cherry Orchard.* They were similar in power and scope to the impact of the early French Impressionists on modern art. With their daring disregard for Aristotelian form, their unique aesthetic, their brilliant vision, and their universal themes, they paved the way for twentieth-century modern drama. Writers around the world from so many different cultures and traditions claim Chekhov as their first and foremost influence. His plays are the most frequently translated and widely produced dramas throughout the world today. They are second only to Shakespeare. These plays are all the more remarkable in that they are the work of a modest man who — in addition to the theater — devoted his life to so many other endeavors. He had very little faith in his abilities as a dramatist, and he knew at a very early age that his life would be short.

In a letter to Tikhonov dated February 22, 1892, Chekhov himself offers a brief, amusing overview of his life:

> Do you need my biography? All right, here it is. I was born in Taganrog in 1860. I graduated from Taganrog Grammar School in 1879. In 1884 I graduated from the medical school of Moscow University. In 1888 I received the Pushkin Prize. In 1890 I made a journey to Sakhalin, across Siberia and returned by sea. In 1891, I completed a tour of Europe, where I drank excellent wine and ate oysters. . . . I began to write in 1879 for the journal "The Dragon Fly." My collected works are: *Motley Stories*, *In the Twilight*, *Tales*, *Gloomy People*, and a novel, *The Duel*. I have also sinned in the realm of drama, although in moderation. I have been translated into all languages with the exception of foreign ones. However, I have already been translated into German, a long time ago. The Czechs and Serbs also approve of me, and the French don't think too badly of me, either. I experienced the mysteries of love at the age of thirteen. With my colleagues, both medical and literary, I remain on excellent terms. I am a bachelor. I would like a pension. I still practice medicine, to the extent that, in the summertime, I even perform an autopsy or two, although I haven't done one now in two, three years. Among writers, my preference is Tolstoy. . . . However, all this is nonsense. Write whatever you like. If you have no facts, substitute something lyrical.

GRANDPARENTS, PARENTS, AND EARLY MEMORIES

Chekhov was born in 1860, in a southern Russian town on the Sea of Azov. He was the son of a shopkeeper. His father's father was a serf of the Voronezh province. He had purchased the freedom of his family in 1841, twenty years before Russia's abolition of serfdom. By dint of hard labor, Chekhov's peasant grandfather, Yegor Chekhov, managed to save 3,500 rubles. He did this to purchase the freedom of his eight-member family at the rate of 500 rubles per head. His master threw one of Yegor's daughters into the bargain "for free."

Pavel Yegorovich, Chekhov's father, opened his own grocery shop in Taganrog. He required the services in the store of his six children: Aleksandr, Nikolai, Anton, Maria (Masha), Ivan, and Mikhail. It was in this grocery store that the vivid scenes of Chekhov's early life played themselves out. These included long hours of labor, limited opportunity for school preparation, and mandatory practice for church choir conducted by his father, which frequently began before dawn. Chekhov's father often beat the children — Lopakhin's description in the opening scene of *The Cherry Orchard* of the blows he received at his father's hand is painfully reminiscent of Chekhov's own experience. The memoirs of Aleksandr, Chekhov's eldest brother, depict, however, a close and lively family life among the siblings during these early years. They were filled with parlor theatricals and practical jokes. These were engendered, authored, and enacted by Anton himself, as an antidote to paternal tyranny. It was in these early years that the humorous muse — and the love of theater — was born in Chekhov.

As a youth, he delighted in stealing away to attend the provincial theater with his brothers. Together, they saw Shakespeare, Hugo, Schiller, and other European classics. He even played a role in Gogol's *Inspector General* in a local amateur production. Translations of *Hamlet* and *Macbeth* were among the first books he owned, as well as Goethe's *Faust*. He frequented the public library and read voraciously — Schopenhauer, Hugo, Cervantes, Goncharov, Turgenev, Belinsky. From his readings, he gained an appreciation of the European heroic tradition. Turgenev's essay "Don Quixote and Hamlet" made a strong impression on him. From the nineteenth-century Russian novel, he gained an appreciation of the Russian protagonist known as the "superfluous man": He was the well-born, well-educated gentlemen who tries in vain to effect change in his society.

THE SEVENTIES: COMING OF AGE

The main event of the 1870s for Chekhov, his second decade, was the relocation of his family. His father's business in Taganrog failed. The bankrupt Pavel Yegorovich fled with his family to Moscow in 1876, leaving Anton behind to face the creditors and complete his studies. For three brief years, Chekhov was completely on his own. While he planned for a medical career, he developed a passion for writing. In 1877–78, he sent a number of short comedic stories and sketches to his brother Aleksandr in Moscow. Alexsandr submitted them for publication. Among them also was a full-length play. Some literary historians speculate that the lost manuscript, purportedly entitled *Fatherless*, was an exorcism of the paternal demons that haunted Chekhov in his early years. In later life, remarkably, Chekhov forgave his father. His only form of rebellion against his pious parent was his rejection of organized religion. Chekhov took responsibility for supporting his parents and siblings throughout his life. In the meantime, though, he dreamed of when he could be close to the "real" theater in Moscow and make his own mark.

TO MOSCOW

When Chekhov arrived on the Moscow scene in 1879 to join his parents in their poor basement flat, he did so with a plan to study medicine. He enrolled at Moscow University. However, he was determined to write serious work for the theater. At nineteen, he already possessed attributes that would serve him well. Among these were an inspired sense of humor, an exposure to classical drama and literature, some amateur experience, and a passion for serious theater. The problem lay not with Chekhov but with the Russian theater. In the 1880s, the Russian theater was stagnating, as Nemirovich-Danchenko, one of the future cofounders of the Moscow Art Theatre, lamented. The 1880s saw the Maly at the height of its fame, but even so, its offerings had become stale and conventional. Most of the repertoires of Moscow and St. Petersburg theaters consisted of foreign classics, Ostrovsky reruns, the few Russian classics that existed, melodramas, farces and numerous vaudevilles, both in translation and imitations by contemporary Russian writers. As for the development of new Russian plays, there were several writers-in-residence at the Maly. It was their task to write expressly for the company's leading actors and actresses. Even so, these were not leading dramatists of the day. Moreover, there was no artistic leadership. The theater was run by a government-appointed administrator, not an artist, and the stage director had no creative power or function.

According to Nemirovich, there were no visionaries on the horizon to lead the Russian theater into new artistic territory. Nor was there any system of identifying, nurturing, and developing serious new dramatists for the stage. To Nemirovich's own complaints about the Maly, Chekhov added his own observations about the other Moscow theaters. These included the mediocrity of the new playwrights, the low level of production values, and the uneducated, ill-prepared, and often inebriated actors. The stagnant Russian theater of the 1880s was ready for new forms and new voices. It was a void that would soon be filled . . . by a new young playwright and a new theater.

PLATONOV

Young Chekhov, compelled to support his studies and his family, began to write sketches for humorous journals. Meanwhile, he plunged into the writing of his first full-length play. This was a melodrama (the untitled, unfinished work now known as *Platonov*), which he ultimately sent to the Maly.

In form, it bore the influence of Turgenev's *A Month in the Country*. It had the same country-estate setting and familiar country types (landowners, doctors, eligible young ladies, and the like). In content, however, it is a bold and deliberate composite of numerous classical portraits. Chekhov had culled these from all the Russian and European literature he had been reading so avidly. The character of Platonov is first and foremost drawn in the tradition of Don Juan. He is the reckless womanizer who attracts us and repels us at the same time with his seductive charm and passion for life, and who is punished in the end. Equally, he is Hamlet in Russian translation (complete with monologues) — ineffective, brooding, erratic, sometimes cruel. Platonov is also a descendant of the romantic Byronic antihero celebrated in nineteenth-century Russian novels. He is like Pechorin of Lermontov's *A Hero of Our Times*, handsome, moody, unstable, aloof, disenchanted. He acts only to relieve the tedium of life or to avenge himself on the society he despises. There is also in Platonov a little of Pushkin's *Eugene Onegin* — that proud young nobleman, self-centered and cruel in love. There is also in Platonov an aspect of Chatsky from Griboedov's social satire *Wit Works Woe*. He is the social conscience of the Russian intellectual, railing at society's injustices, knowing he can do nothing to change them.

In summary, Platonov was the legacy of many literary personae, six portraits combined. The neophyte dramatist Chekhov was so passionately intent on creating a heroic type for the Russian stage that he attempted to combine all past portrayals into one. He was stung by the rejection of this youthful work by the Maly Theater, where he had been intent on making his debut. He turned to the writing of short stories for the next few years while he finished his medical studies.

IVANOV

It was in 1887 that Chekhov received a commission to write a full-length play from the Korsh. This was one of the first commercial theaters established since the czar's edict allowing commercial theaters. At last, a point of dramatic focus had presented itself, and a prestigious Moscow theater had given him *carte blanche*. Here was the opportunity to make his mark as a serious dramatist. He could accomplish onstage what Pushkin, Lermontov, and Turgenev before him had accomplished, to create a "type of literary significance" for the theater, but in a new, original incarnation. In a burst of excitement, Chekhov wrote his new play, *Ivanov*, in ten days. He delivered it to the Korsh, confident in its success. Imagine, then, his bewilderment when it was met with wildly divergent critical and audience response. There were reviews of praise and condemnation, and even fist fights in the theater lobby. What frustrated Chekhov most was his failure, once again, to create an original heroic type for the Russian theater. He was told that Ivanov came across either as an unsympathetic scoundrel or as a rehash of the Russian "superfluous man," a figure from nineteenth-century Russian literature. This confounded Chekhov, and it turned him off serious playwriting for eight years.

However controversial, *Ivanov* had a great impact on the Moscow theater scene. It enhanced Chekhov's reputation as a successful writer. Chekhov, however, was dismayed by what he perceived to be a misunderstanding by the critics and the public of his serious dramatic intentions. They also seemed to misunderstand his central character, Ivanov, a portrait of a "man of the eighties," a liberal idealist who could not effect social change. Chekhov's first response was to turn the blame upon himself and his shortcomings. Clearly, he must be a failure as a dramatist, he thought. "Apparently it's too early for me to begin writing plays," he wrote to his publisher on December 20, 1888.

DISAPPOINTMENT AND SUCCESS

Nonetheless, the decade of the 1880s, the Moscow period, marks the period of greatest productivity in Chekhov's literary career. It also saw his remarkable rise to fame and popularity among the Moscow *literati*. From 1880–87, he contributed almost 400 humorous sketches and short stories to numerous literary publications of the day. He used a variety of *noms de plume*, including "Antosha Chekhonte." Among the stories were "My Brother's Brother," "A Doctor without Patients," and "A Man without a

Spleen." Then, in 1884, he received his medical degree. He installed his family in a modest town house on Sadovo-Kudrinskaya Street in Moscow. There the young Dr. Chekhov lived with his large family, practicing medicine and literature at the same time. His fame grew. He acquired a noted publisher, Suvorin. His stories began to be published in collections to widespread popularity. Meanwhile, despite what he perceived his failure as a serious dramatist, Chekhov turned to a dramatic form that came easily to him: the vaudeville.

"LIKE OIL FROM THE DEPTHS OF THE BAKU"

In the 1880s, the vaudeville was one of the most popular forms on the Moscow stage. This popular, eclectic, low-comedy genre had its origins in Paris street theater. The vaudeville found its way to the Russian stage in the 1830s where it gained popularity. This was mostly because, as pure entertainment, it was the only form that could get past the stern Imperial censorship implemented by Czar Nicholas I. An indication of its popularity is that 40 percent of the repertoire at the Aleksandrinsky Theater in St. Petersburg during the 1840s consisted of vaudevilles. Some were translated from French and German. Others were Russian versions based on a fairly fixed formula according to conventions. These included stock settings and characters, formulaic plots, rapid-paced action, all culminating in a happy ending. By the time Chekhov arrived on the theater scene in the 1880s, the Russian vaudeville, a popular form for over half a century, was so overused that it was in a state of ossification.

Bruised by his unsuccessful attempts at writing serious drama, Chekhov eagerly turned to the vaudeville. From 1886–89, he wrote seven short plays that he classified in the vaudeville genre. Their subtitles — farce, monologue, one-act play, and so on — varied. *The Bear* (1888) would be the most popular. It became a personal favorite of Tolstoy, and it earned Chekhov more money than any of his short stories. Equally popular was *The Proposal* (1888), a favorite of the czar. He arranged for its performance at his summer residence at Czarskoe Selo in 1889. These vaudevilles were joined by *On the Harmful Effects of Tobacco* (1886), *Swan Song* (1887), *The Tragedian in Spite of Himself* (1889), and *The Wedding* (1889). They seemed to pour from him as effortlessly as "oil from the depths of the Baku," as he put it in a letter to his publisher Suvorin dated December 23, 1888. They also placed Chekhov stage center in the Moscow theater scene. They captivated the public. They also elicited the critical recognition he had craved.

Moreover, Chekhov managed to create innovative variations to the vaudeville's conventions, while still preserving its ability to entertain. He took stock character types (like the inept suitor in *The Proposal*) and, either through parody or subversion, humanized them. He created new types as well — such as the pathetic hen-pecked schoolteacher in *Tobacco*. He brought a new sense of the absurd to the vaudeville through exaggerated behavior and physical actions (in *The Bear*). He introduced innovative usage of language. Indeed, he endowed the vaudevilles with a Russian flavor. Through this experimentation, Chekhov reaffirmed the classical strength of comedy as a vehicle of serious social commentary and thought. He satirized contemporary topics, poking fun at feminism, the greedy middle class, the ineptitude and self-importance of government institutions, to mention only a few. Above all, he introduced into the vaudeville genre an element of the tragicomic. Ironically, then, Chekhov made his mark on the Moscow theater scene with a comedic form that came easily to him, not the tragic form he struggled to create. In doing so, he succeeded in elevating the vaudeville into an art form, and he provided supreme entertainment as well as insight into the human condition.

In a three-year period he experienced whirlwind popularity as a vaudeville writer. In this period he also published more than 300 of his short stories. This placed Chekhov in the front ranks of Russian writers by the age of twenty-eight. In 1888, he was awarded the prestigious Pushkin Prize by the Imperial Academy of Sciences in Petersburg. In

1889, he was elected to the Society of Lovers of Russian Literature. Nonetheless, this popularity could not assuage the frustration at not yet finding his serious dramatic voice. On October 10, 1888, he wrote to Suvorin, "Everything I have written, everything I received the prize for, will live no more than ten years in people's memories." He harbored resentment for the success the humorous muse brought him so easily, and for the difficulty he had in the serious vein. Meanwhile, Chekhov struggled to rewrite *Ivanov* for its St. Petersburg production in 1889. Even though the rewriting process brought critical success, still it did not satisfy him. Clearly, he was frustrated that somehow the serious dramatist in him had not yet found a voice. In any case, he felt the public was not ready to hear it.

THE WOOD DEMON: A COMEDY IN FOUR ACTS

Smarting from the controversy surrounding *Ivanov*, and ever eager to please the audience and the critics, Chekhov next wrote a long romantic comedy. *The Wood Demon* (a "comedy in four acts") premiered on December 27, 1889, at the Abramov Theater in Moscow. With its uniform critical failure, Chekhov's worst fears were reconfirmed regarding his dramaturgical skills, and he forbade its publication. Indeed, the literary committee of a St. Petersburg theater advised him to stick to writing stories. It was the response to this third full-length work that drove Chekhov to bring the Moscow period of his life to an end.

Chekhov was bored by the superficialities of fame, peeved by the Moscow literary scene, and unfulfilled by his success as a humorous writer. In particular, he was wounded by the criticism of his plays and frustrated by what he saw to be his failures. The death of his brother, Nikolai, of consumption, grieved him and made him fearful for his own health. So Chekhov sought an escape from his dramaturgical efforts. He wished to purify himself of the only source of bitterness in his life to date: the theater.

A JOURNEY TO SAKHALIN

In 1890, Chekhov made the historic journey across Siberia to the island of Sakhalin off the Pacific Coast. His aim was to study the penal colonies and penal codes. In seeking to give expression to another side of himself — the doctor and humanitarian — the journey concluding the Moscow period was nonetheless born of spiritual need for Chekhov the serious playwright. This need was finding a voice even before the opening of *The Wood Demon*. It was a journey that provides a special landmark for Chekhov the dramatist — the beginning of a six-year hiatus in serious full-length playwriting. On this journey and in the years of personal growth to follow, Chekhov gained a vital feeling of personal freedom. This, more than the acquiring of technique and skill, permitted the four major plays to be born.

THE MELIKHOVO PERIOD: 1892–99

The decade of the 1890s when Chekhov was in his thirties marks the turning point from humorist to serious dramatist.

His arduous journey by land to Sakhalin, and back by sea, took over a year and had a significant spiritual impact on him. The separation from Moscow life was crucial in giving him the perspective he knew he needed for his development as a dramatist. Once back in Russia, wanderlust overtook him again, and he left for Western Europe. Finally, in 1892, he fulfilled a dream. He purchased an "estate," called Melikhovo (actually, a picturesque *dacha* on several hundred acres of land) about sixty miles southeast of Moscow. Here he chose to do his writing away from Moscow and his family. They subsequently joined him there nonetheless.

Once installed in Melikhovo, he plunged into community activities. He practiced medicine from his tiny "estate," joining vigorously in the fight against the cholera epidemic. He built schools with his own funds, and he started other programs to benefit the peasant population. During this period, his productivity in short story writing decreased to a handful per year.

Still, it was a gratifying period for Chekhov. The presence of nature, which he romanticized in his plays of the '80s, was now a real part of his life. Many of his young artist and literary friends flocked there from Moscow to enjoy the idyllic setting and to walk through the woods. The beauty of the surroundings, the distraction of the young visitors, and the whirlwind of the community activities further served to distract him from his ever-present illness.

THE TRANSFORMATION OF AN ARTIST

There was a seven-year hiatus between the opening of *The Wood Demon* in 1889, Chekhov's third full-length play and a critical failure, and the writing of *The Seagull* (the first of what would be called the four major plays). During that time, a variety of factors contributed to Chekhov's personal and artistic growth. He had a sense of personal feeling gained by taking leave of his family and Moscow. The journey he took to Sakhalin on a humanitarian mission influenced him deeply. Meanwhile, he was nourished by his retreat to Melikhovo and the Russian countryside he loved. The practice of medicine as a country doctor nurtured him as well. In this period he pursued his personal relationships with artist friends, which served as material for his plays. As his health failed, he had a sense of the finiteness of life. He had a sense of responsibility as an author of the *fin de siècle* and a new centennial. He also sensed the decline of Russia, paralleling his own decline. In that period, his productivity diminished to the point where he wrote only one more vaudeville and a dozen or so short stories from 1891–95. More importantly, it was a time of personal and artistic transformation, which yielded the four major plays he would write from 1896 to 1904.

THE FIRST OF THE FOUR MAJOR PLAYS

In a letter to Suvorin dated October 21, 1895, Chekhov wrote the following:

> Can you imagine — I am writing a play . . . not without pleasure, though I abuse the conventions of the stage terribly. It's a comedy, there are . . . four acts, landscapes (view over a lake); a great deal of conversation about literature, little action, tons of love.

Nowhere in the letter does he comment on the source of inspiration for his first major play, *The Seagull*. This letter, in fact, is the first mention of it. Yet it must have already been taking shape in his dramatic imagination.

Set on an estate in the countryside by a lake, the play tells the story of an aspiring young avant-garde playwright, Treplev. He wants to stage his new play to impress his mother and her lover Trigorin, an established short story writer. Treplev enlists his young lover, Nina, an aspiring young actress, to perform in his play. Covering three ensuing years of their lives and the tragic events that unfold after that fateful performance one innocent summer night, the play deals with love, art, nature, death, and, above all, the question of what it means to be an artist. It details the risks one must take to create "new forms" for the theater, as Treplev calls them. It also looks at the price one must pay and the lengths to which one must go to be an artist, including the destruction of one's self and one's loved ones.

For his play, Chekhov clearly drew upon events in the lives of his artist friends who were visiting Melikhovo. These included the suicidal artist Levitan, and no less than three young women named Lydia, all of whom were hopelessly in love with Chekhov at the time. Indeed, there is the suggestion that Treplev and Trigorin, the two writers in the play, are aspects of Chekhov the writer himself. In Chekhov's ensuing correspondence, behind a tone of self-deprecation and flippancy, there is a sense of excitement that he had written something new.

THE SEAGULL: A RESOUNDING FAILURE

The ill-fated story of *The Seagull*'s first production is legendary in theater history. By September, it was too late to be included in the prestigious Maly Theater's repertoire in Moscow for the current season, where Chekhov had hoped to have it staged. Instead, it was offered to the Aleksandrinsky Theater in St. Petersburg, where Chekhov's reputation as a writer of vaudevilles was well known. Amusingly enough, the play made it past the Imperial censor. (One of the few changes requested was that a line indicating that Treplev's mother, the actress Arkadina, was "smoking, drinking, and living openly with that novelist" be struck from the script!) Unhappily, the play, directed by the theater's stage manager, had only nine days of rehearsal, on the fourth day of which the actress playing Nina was replaced by the well-known actress Vera Kommisarzhevskaya. She was, according to Chekhov, the only one in the cast who had any sense of his play. Thus in an atmosphere of artistic disunity, ill-preparation, and utter dread, Chekhov attended the disastrous opening night on October 17, 1896. After hearing the boisterous, derisive laughter in Act One during Nina's poetic speech in Treplev's play, Chekhov took refuge in the dressing rooms and ultimately fled the theater, vowing never again to write another play.

AN HISTORIC MEETING

While Chekhov was nursing his dramaturgical wounds, a momentous dinner meeting took place at the Slavyansky Bazaar, a famous Moscow hotel, on June 22, 1897. Playwright/critic/dramaturg Vladimir Nemirovich-Danchenko and actor/director Konstantin Alekseev, otherwise known as Stanislavsky, had a famous meeting. Out of that historic eighteen-hour conversation, the Moscow Art Theatre was born.

It was a theater dedicated to rebellion against the highly styled theater of the nineteenth century. Its two founders set out to establish new standards for work. They wanted to create a theater that would match and even surpass the Maly. They sought to create a true ensemble theater based on a method of realistic acting and production. Stanislavsky's aim was a new acting style based on truth and feeling. Nemirovich wanted to encourage and develop new writing for the theater. Together they solicited resources and attracted a vibrant new company of young actors. A number of these actors were Nemirovich's own acting students.

CHEKHOV AND THE MOSCOW ART THEATRE

First and foremost, their goal was to produce *The Seagull*, a play by the new playwright, Anton Chekhov, in their inaugural season. Nemirovich admired the play passionately. He went so far as to say that it was the only new play that excited him and that Chekhov was the only contemporary dramatist of value.

Chekhov was approached, but he was reluctant. He had been traumatized by the negative criticism of *The Seagull*'s first production at the Aleksandrinsky Theater the previous year. Fortunately, Nemirovich persisted, and finally Chekhov relented. The production was directed by Stanislavsky. He also played Trigorin (a performance of which Chekhov was highly critical) opposite a passionate young actress and student of Nemirovich named Olga Knipper. (She was later to be Chekhov's leading lady and his wife.) The second production in the theater's first season, it opened on December 17, 1898, to ecstatic audience response and critical praise. Knipper reports in her memoirs that so excited were the cast members on opening night that they took valerian drops to stay calm.

How could the play that had received such poor reviews only two years before in St. Petersburg have become so huge a success in Moscow? The answer, of course, is by virtue of the passion that the members of this young company had for Chekhov's work. It also was a result of their understanding and appreciation of its newness and its aesthetic. With that opening, the Moscow Art Theatre became "Chekhov's Theater," and *The Seagull* became its emblem — even to this day.

Chekhov never quite recovered from the fiasco of *The Seagull*'s initial premiere. He lapsed into a new kind of detached anxiety about playwriting. He was unable to trust the affirmation of this unexpected, exhilarating triumph and the promise it held for the future. Even though he ultimately wrote three more masterpieces, he would never overcome his sensitivity to the vicissitudes of the theater. In writing a play about a seagull that was shot and eventually stuffed, could he have been anticipating what might happen to him as a playwright, once he ventured to write in a new form?

DRAMATURGICAL MYSTERY

Even before the Moscow Art Theatre produced *The Seagull* and well before its first, provincial production, Chekhov had already written his next play, *Uncle Vanya*.

Of all the major plays, *Uncle Vanya* is the one least mentioned in Chekhov's correspondence. Indeed, the actual date of the writing of *Uncle Vanya* remains a mystery in literary history. One suspects this was deliberately created by its author who was protecting himself from what he perceived to be his chronic failure as a serious dramatist. Most speculate that it was written sometime between November 1895, after the completion of the first draft of *The Seagull*, and December 2, 1896, when Chekhov first mentions it to his publisher. "My plays are being printed," he complains, "with amazing slowness . . . two full-length plays are not yet included in any collection: *The Seagull*, known to you, and *Uncle Vanya*, unknown to anyone on earth . . . "

Uncle Vanya was again set in the Russian countryside with an ensemble cast of characters. It tells the story of the arrival of an eminent professor for a summer sojourn on the family estate. There its owner (Vanya) and a country doctor (Astrov) fall in love with the professor's beautiful young wife. Whiling the summer away in fruitless love intrigue, the characters struggle with the realization that their dreams and passions will never be fulfilled. They are trapped in this country life that is both a haven and a prison. With autumn, aging, and the shadow of death encroaching on them, they realize that work is their only salvation. The play begins and ends with an unanswered question: "Will we be remembered?"

There was a second reason for Chekhov's reticence about his new play. The text of *Uncle Vanya* is a skillful reworking of *The Wood Demon*, the earlier work whose critical failure in 1889 had wounded him so deeply. The dramaturgical transformation is dazzling, demonstrating Chekhov's acquired skills as a dramatist. He reworked the plot and reimagined the characters, altering the tone from a romantic comedy to a deeper tragicomedy. Also of significance is the metamorphosis of the play's setting. The Russian countryside is transformed from an imaginary place of frivolous romance to a place where the real hardships of provincial life and the spiritual isolation are now depicted. This transformation comes from Chekhov's life in Melikhovo. It reflects his experiences both as a landowner and a country doctor. Chekhov's romanticization of nature in the 1880s had deepened into a broader perception of nature. It was now not only a place of beauty but also of mystery and even danger. It was a place of forces beyond the control and comprehension of man.

A SECOND SUCCESS

The first productions of *Uncle Vanya* took place in 1897 in several provincial Russian theaters with positive results. At first, the Imperial censors banned its production. They expressed dismay that anyone would aim a gun at an eminent Russian professor. Despite everything, however, approval was finally granted.

Still reeling with the success of *The Seagull*, Stanislavsky and Nemirovich pressured Chekhov to give them *Uncle Vanya* for their second

(1899) season. Unfortunately, Chekhov had already promised it to the Maly Theater for its first professional production. As it happened, however, the Maly demanded radical rewrites of the play. Chekhov refused. In the end, he gave the rights to Nemirovich and Stanislavsky. The play opened at the Moscow Art Theatre on October 26, 1899. Olga Knipper played Yelena. Stanislavsky played Astrov and was the production's director. Though reviews were mixed, the audiences were very moved. It was considered the second great success in the collaboration of Chekhov and the Moscow Art Theatre.

While these productions of Chekhov's plays by the Moscow Art Theatre may have been successful, still there were artistic tensions. Working in the theater, and with Stanislavsky, had always been a source of anxiety for Chekhov. This was true even though he was fascinated by all aspects of preproduction. Indeed, he insisted on being informed regarding all aspects of rehearsals, demanding reports even when he was away from Moscow. As for Stanislavsky, he was, as usual, overextended. He was working both as actor and director in other productions that second season, as well as managing his family's factories. Consequently, he frequently missed rehearsals. Nemirovich had to see to it that Stanislavsky learned his lines, that he not knock props and furniture around during rehearsals, and that he not indulge in uncalled for theatrics. Displeased, Chekhov wrote to Olga on October 4, 1899: "When Stanislavsky directs, he's an artist, but when he acts, he's just a rich young merchant who wants to dabble in art."

In March 1897, following the completion of *Uncle Vanya*, Chekhov experienced his most violent hemorrhage to date, causing him to face the seriousness of his condition. His doctors urged him to move to the South. With reluctance, Chekhov gave up his medical practice at Melikhovo. He started to spend longer periods of time in Yalta, convalescing, the result being that he was unable to attend the Moscow Art Theatre openings of either *The Seagull* or *Uncle Vanya*. It was not until the spring of 1900, to celebrate the centennial and to honor their beloved author, that the Moscow Art Theatre toured their production of *Uncle Vanya* to Yalta. They performed it there for him before an audience that included Rachmaninov, Tolstoy, Bunin, Kuprin, Gorky, and others. It was an exciting time. Chekhov entertained the troupe nightly. He was exhilarated, exhausted, and in love once again with the theater. At the production's close, the Art Theatre troupe brought the swing and the bench from Act One of *Vanya* and placed it in Chekhov's garden near his orchard of almond trees.

THE THREE SISTERS: A PLAY FOR OLGA

Now considered the Art Theatre's playwright-in-residence, Chekhov's bond with the company was further strengthened by a blossoming romance with its leading lady, Olga Knipper. A former student of Nemirovich, this fiery young actress had played the roles of Arkadina and Yelena. Chekhov now considered her the "interpreter" of his roles. Chekhov and Olga had become lovers in the summer of 1900. After she returned to Moscow in August to prepare for the upcoming theater season, Chekhov sat down and wrote the play that would be the first written expressly for the Moscow Art Theatre, *The Three Sisters*. The role of Masha was meant for Olga.

The Three Sisters tells the story of the Prozorov family. The three sisters and a brother live in a remote provincial town. Here, they come to terms with their hopes for love, success, and their ultimate dream of moving back to Moscow, the city of their childhood. In the course of the play, which spans three years of their lives, each of the Prozorovs faces acute disappointment and severe loss, and they achieve none of their dreams. All the philosophizing of the men they admire and their visions for a shining future have come to naught. As the eldest sister, Olga, realizes, "we shall vanish, we shall disappear without a trace." At the play's end, like the characters in *Uncle Vanya*, the three sisters find that the only way to live is to endure . . . and to work.

It was Chekhov's most ambitious work to date with the largest number of characters and the most complex plot. He struggled with the writing, continuing to express self-doubt as to his dramatic skills.

Chekhov attended the first reading of the new play by the company in the fall of 1900. Discouraged by the perplexed response of the company, frustrated with anxiety over the upcoming rehearsals and the requested rewrites, and plagued by his ill health, Chekhov retreated to Nice. From there he mailed the rewrites to Nemirovich. He wrote to Olga daily, begging for details of the rehearsal process. He was wary of Stanislavsky, who was again directing. According to Chekhov, Stanislavsky's tendency was to interpret Chekhov's plays as tragedies and to pace them slowly. This frustrated Chekhov deeply. At the eleventh hour, Stanislavsky took over the role of Vershinin, under Nemirovich's direction. Meanwhile, Chekhov had fled from Nice to Italy, and he was unreachable on opening night, January 31, 1901. Indeed, the news of the triumphant opening did not reach him till after he returned to Yalta in February.

On May 25, 1901, following the January opening of *The Three Sisters*, Chekhov and Olga were married in a church outside Moscow. Owing either to Chekhov's anxieties or his love of practical jokes, the couple planned a reception where family and friends awaited them. They then deliberately didn't appear; they went to a church alone at a separate location. They were married with no witnesses from the family to whom he had been devoted all his life.

THE ART THEATRE IN ASCENDANCE

Now considered the rising star in the Russian theater, the Moscow Art Theatre received, in 1901, a heavy subsidy from Morozov. This would allow the troupe to move into a modern building with updated equipment. Also in 1901, thanks to Chekhov's persuasive efforts, the young playwright Maxim Gorky began working on his first plays, *Small People* and *The Lower Depths*. When they were done, he sent them to the Art Theatre. By 1902, the Art Theatre's supremacy was established, with Chekhov's three plays continuously performed in the repertoire.

Olga's tragic miscarriage in February 1902 kept her out of the season in the spring. Fortunately, after a five-month convalescence with Chekhov, she was back in Moscow, performing with the company.

THE CHERRY ORCHARD: THE FINAL PLAY

Meanwhile, Stanislavsky, Nemirovich, and Olga pressured him continually for a new play. In 1903, Chekhov's health was in such a steep decline that he could barely write more than a few lines a day. In Yalta, lonely and ailing, he nonetheless struggled to write the play he'd promised Olga, to cheer her up after her loss. Its title — *The Cherry Orchard.* Whereas his other major plays took two months each to write, he struggled with this play for months.

Finally, he sent the manuscript from Yalta in October 1903. Stanislavsky organized a reading immediately. He then telegrammed Chekhov with his ecstatic congratulations, reporting how the company had wept when they read it. This infuriated Chekhov, who had subtitled the play "a comedy." He insisted on coming to Moscow and attended rehearsals in order to keep an eye on Stanislavsky.

Rehearsals were a torture for him. He remonstrated Stanislavsky continually over his elaborate direction and insistence on overloading the production with gratuitous sound effects. Ever eager for good reviews, Stanislavsky decided to schedule the opening night on January 17, 1904 — Chekhov's birthday. He wanted to celebrate the twenty-fifth anniversary of Chekhov's work as a writer as well. Stanislavsky also hoped that the sight of the ailing playwright would soften any potential critical blows. The reluctant Chekhov had to be coerced onto the stage, coughing, after the third act. There was a forty-five-minute opening night testimonial. He could barely stand, and he was embarrassed by the elaborate wreaths and gifts. Despite the audience's emotional response to his much-weakened appearance, Stanislavsky's plan was not altogether successful. Again, the critical reviews were mixed.

THE LONG SHADOW DARKENING

The Cherry Orchard was by far the longest in the writing of any of the four major plays. It took ten months, due largely to the constant interruptions of visitors and his declining health. "My darling," he wrote to Olga on October 12, 1903, "how hard it was for me to write that play." The long shadow of his illness was darkening.

That Chekhov knew this would be his last is perhaps the source of the play's inspiration. He felt the end of his own life approaching, but he also felt keenly the turning tides of a new century. He recognized, in a nondidactic way, that it was the end of an era for Russia and the dawn of a new one. Even in his initial vision of the play — an old lady, an old manservant, an orchard all in white, and ladies in white dresses — the elements of the old, the new, the end, the beginning are central. This play would be somewhat different from the previous three. As Chekhov pointed out, there was no gun, no doctor, and no love. These elements were consistently present in all his other plays. Perhaps this insistence that the play be called a comedy reflected his wish to end his literary oeuvre with a vision of optimism. In the subtle mixture of comedic and dramatic tones of the play, he was also making his own sober prediction about the future.

In this final play, Lyubov Ranevskaya, a landowner, returns from abroad. She and her brother confront the necessity of either paying the mortgage (long in arrears) or selling their crumbling family estate, which had been in their family for generations. Chekhov chose his characters carefully, each representing a different segment of a changing social order. There were, among others, the impoverished but elegant landowners Lyubov and Gaev; the capitalist Lopakhin who wants to buy the estate in order to cut down the cherry orchard and build summer cottages for renters; and Lyubov's daughter, Anya, and a young revolutionary student, Trofimov, who represent various points of view of the new generation. There is also a governess, Charlotta, of unknown nationality, representing the displaced people in a society in flux, and an ancient servant, Firs. He is the last servant on the estate, one who had refused his freedom from his masters in the Emancipation of 1861.

In *The Cherry Orchard*, Chekhov saw a dying Russia through the eyes of a dying man. "Good-bye old life, hello new life," cry out the new generation. They are represented by Lyubov's daughter, Anya, as the family is finally forced to abandon their estate, while no one knows what the future will bring. There is only the unknown, the mysterious, represented by the strange sound of a breaking string far in the distance — the most haunting premonition in all of Chekhov's work.

THE FINAL BOW

From February until October 1903, as he struggled to write *The Cherry Orchard*, Olga, Stanislavsky, and Nemirovich pressured him. They may not have realized how seriously ill Chekhov was. In fact, there were days when he could only write a few lines, owing to the increased feeling of weakness, headaches, and the constant coughing. Thankfully, he was able to complete it, and *The Cherry Orchard* opened on his final birthday: January 17, 1904.

Three months following the premiere of *The Cherry Orchard*, in response to his declining health, Chekhov's doctors sent him abroad to Germany with Olga Knipper. They took up residence at a spa in Badenweiler. The story of his death and burial reads like one of his own later, ironic stories. On the night of July 2, Chekhov asked his wife and the German doctor for a glass of champagne. After drinking it, he said: "Ich sterbe."

He died peacefully. Ironically, his body was shipped to Russia by train in a car marked "oysters" (one of his favorite indulgences). The train was met in the Moscow station by a military band. It was not for Chekhov, but for a high-ranking military official on the same train. He was buried in the cemetery of the Novodevichy Monastery, the burial site of the mother of Olga, Masha, and Irina in *The Three Sisters*.

To the very end, he felt misunderstood as a dramatist, despite all the accolades his major plays had brought him. Weeks before his death, he wrote to Olga about *The Cherry Orchard*, lamenting Stanislavsky's interpretation of the play as a tragedy instead of a comedy, as he had intended.

OLGA AFTER ANTON

After Chekhov's death, Olga remained with the Moscow Art Theatre, performing all the roles in her husband's plays into her eighties. A famous story reports that, after she retired from the stage, one evening she was sitting in a theater box during a performance of *The Three Sisters*. She was displeased with the actress's interpretation of the role her husband had written for her, and she was heard to call out Masha's lines from her seat in the auditorium.

THE ART THEATRE AFTER CHEKHOV

In the decade following Chekhov's death, the Art Theatre struggled with many vicissitudes, including the loss of Gorky as successor to its playwright-in-residence Chekhov. They also lost Morozov's financial support and experienced critical failures. There was growing tension between its founders, Stanislavsky and Nemirovich. The company's first European tour in 1906 launched its international reputation just at a crucial moment when it was in danger of collapse. A system of studios within the company was introduced, decentralizing the artistic leadership even more. By the time of the 1917 Bolshevik Revolution, the Art Theatre was at its lowest ebb, and in 1921, its subsidy was threatened. In an effort to survive, it decided to tour Berlin, Paris, and the United States from 1922 through 1924.

The tour, however, only further depleted the energies of its leaders and actors. Nonetheless, it kept the theater's artistic spirit alive and brought Chekhov's plays to new audiences. It also brought the Art

Theatre's acting style to the attention of American audiences and artists. This ultimately changed the course of the American theater. In Moscow, too, the Art Theatre has survived with its internationally renowned theater school and classical repertoire, which still includes all the plays of Anton Chekhov. The Moscow Art Theatre remains one of the leading theaters of the world.

CHEKHOV'S LEGACY

Chekhov's major plays take place in his own times and are set on country estates — or, in the case of *The Three Sisters*, in a grand house in a provincial town. They are inhabited primarily by the landed gentry and other members of the educated and privileged classes. While Chekhov's settings and their inhabitants may have not been new to the Russian theater, his treatments of them were. Seen as a whole, the four major plays had a new and distinct presence all their own on the Russian stage. Clearly, the public, the critics, and the actors of Chekhov's times who saw and performed in his plays recognized their "newness." Despite his agonizing doubts as to his own abilities as a serious dramatist, Chekhov, too, knew that he was writing "new forms."

This "newness" is challenging to define and describe. Chekhov broke free from the conventions of Ostrovskian drama and its standards of plot and characterization, which had influenced the Russian theater since the 1850s. The meaning of the terms "realism" and "naturalism" as applied to Chekhov's plays, which one encounters in literary criticism, can be problematic. This is because the definitions of these terms change with every decade and the appearance of more "new" writers for the stage, whose work challenges us to redefine our terminology. Chekhov himself scoffed at the description of his plays as "realistic." He said that one could hardly surgically remove a nose from a portrait, substitute it with a real one, and still call it art. His contemporaries recognized this newness in the major plays. Stanislavsky and Nemirovich thought Chekhov to be a genius, admiring the freshness and simplicity of the plays. Gorky noted the original-ity of the form and the broad scope of the ideas. Knipper spoke of the remarkable world of the Chekhovian play and how actors loved to live in it.

Chekhov himself put it best when he said he strove to put "life as it is" on the stage. This is what he set out to do in *Ivanov* in the 1880s and had to struggle for two decades to give it expression in the later major plays.

THE NATURE OF THE NEWNESS

The sense of "newness" lay in a unique combination of dramatic ele-ments. First, Chekhov boldly disregarded Aristotelian rules of drama-turgy pertaining to action and character. He used a consistent four-act form with a deliberate lack of strong dramatic plot. There was an ab-sence of a central heroic character, replaced by an ensemble that repre-sented all strata of Russian society. Certainly, there were remarkably rich individual character portrayals. These were alive, detailed, and gracefully drawn. The atmosphere was evoked by a very specific mise-en-scène. Chekhov used the simple details of everyday life, surrounded by the sense of a vaster landscape. He evoked the passage of time, while at the same time creating a very special, unique tragicomic tone.

Second, Chekhov introduced a new "non-Aristotelian" notion of dramatic action, to, as he said, depict "life as it is" on the stage. In the major plays, there are no "Ivanovs" who shot themselves onstage. All significant action takes place offstage, while onstage there is everyday life: arrivals, sojourns, departures, and the trivialities of daily existence. As Chekhov once remarked to the writer Goroditsky, as quoted by Gilles:

> In life, one does not shoot oneself in the head, hang oneself, or de-clare one's passion at every fencepost, and one does not pour out profound thoughts in a constant flow. No, mostly one eats, drinks,

flirts, makes stupid remarks: that is what should be seen on the stage. One must write plays in which people come and go, have dinner, talk about the rain, play cards — not because this is the author's whim but because this is what happens in real life. . . . Nothing must be fitted into a pattern.

Third, Chekhov introduced "living characters" to the Russian stage. His characters were full human portrayals with rich inner lives, emotional and psychological complexities, spirituality, and colorful outward "behavior." For the Moscow Art Theatre, whose founding purpose was to create a new school of acting for the Russian stage, these new plays and characters were ideal.

VISUAL AESTHETIC

Chekhov also brought a strong new visual aesthetic to the Russian stage. His mise-en-scènes are sharp and specific for each of the four acts. He gives time of day, season, climate, light, sound, and the strong presence of nature and the elements. Serving as the backdrop to the details of everyday life, these richly textured settings create a mood, as the story moves from act to act, from exterior to interior — or reverse — as spaces contract, empty, and darken, as weather changes, as time passes. Specific scenic elements, such as a mounted seagull, a samovar, a piano, a clock, or sounds, such as a night watchman knocking, a lonely gun shot, a breaking string, an axe falling against a tree, stand out in sharp relief. Like a Pointillist painter, Chekhov introduced a new aesthetic, one of detail, translucence, and depth. His plays have an evocative atmosphere all their own.

COMEDY OR TRAGEDY, OR BOTH?

Whether Chekhov's plays were comedies (he being alone and adamant in this opinion) or dramas or tragedies, as Stanislavsky maintained, is a topic that has provoked misunderstandings and misinterpretations of Chekhov's plays then and today. The debate was alive throughout the production of the four major plays at the Moscow Art Theatre. It came to a peak during the preparation for the production of *The Cherry Orchard*. Chekhov insisted it was a comedy, but Stanislavsky wanted to direct it for tragic effect. When Stanislavsky pointed out the many references in the text to the characters who speak "in tears," Chekhov retorted that that was not what he meant. Some theater historians maintain that his irritability on this subject was further exacerbated by his worsening health. Perhaps he deliberately titled it a comedy because he knew it was his last work, and he wanted to end his literary oeuvre as such. In the end, one must search to find the intent behind his insistence, to do his plays justice on the stage.

Finding the special tone in a Chekhov play — also referred to by Nemirovich and Stanislavsky as the "Chekhovian" mood or atmosphere — is dealing with both perspectives — the comedic and the tragic. This allows them to be coexistent, rather than mutually exclusive. Indeed, it was the struggle with this disagreement that brought Stanislavsky to the realization that he expressed in *My Life in Art*. He said that the characters in Chekhov's plays do not indulge in their own sorrow but rather reach, as Chekhov did himself, for life, joy, and laughter. They want to live life to its fullest. It is their struggle in face of the insurmountable obstacles in life that is both comedic and tragic at the same time.

For theater artists of every generation, understanding Chekhov the man and his very special vision of life will help to understand why he called his plays comedies and why his plays conclude, as Astrov puts it, with *"finita la commedia!"* The plays are Chekhov's special vision of the comedy of life itself. Thus, the characters live through the tragic events of the play, laughing through their tears, as the stage directions indicate. Meanwhile, the larger worldview — the tragicomedy of life that Chekhov has written — comes to life on the stage.

A PLACE IN HISTORY

How would Chekhov have wished to be placed in dramatic literature? First, as a profoundly modest and self-effacing writer, he repeatedly wrote that he never expected his work to be remembered after his death. His short story writing came easily to him. He never had faith in his abilities as a dramatist, so he had no expectations of immortality. Furthermore, he came from a literary tradition where authors came almost exclusively from the privileged, landowning classes. As the grandson of a serf and the son of a shopkeeper, he was well aware of his humble origins. So imagine how amazed he would be if he knew that his name is now placed among the great Russian authors — Pushkin, Lermontov, Gogol, Turgenev, Tolstoy — whom he so greatly admired. He would be more amazed to know that he is considered his country's greatest playwright, not to mention world famous.

Second, as a writer who repeatedly resisted labels (realism, naturalism, symbolism), he would not want to be categorized. To some extent, one might say that he satirizes the Russian symbolist movement of the day in his treatment of Treplev's play-within-the-play in *The Seagull*. The exotic elements of the symbolist movement fascinated him, and one can argue that there is a strain of symbolism in the four major plays. Nonetheless, one cannot call Chekhov a symbolist writer. Chekhov still defies categorization, despite literary critics' attempts to do so over the past century.

For example, Chekhov's plays, with their nonaction, paved the way for Samuel Beckett's. Nonetheless, Chekhov cannot be considered solely an existentialist (though there may be elements of that philosophy in his plays). He belongs to no school, to no trend or literary tendency. "I write about life as it is," he repeatedly said. So labels such as realism, naturalism, and so forth don't serve Chekhov's work. No, his vision is far broader and deeper. Indeed, consider the wide divergence of contemporary writers and artists who claim Chekhov as their major influence. These include the European playwrights Samuel Beckett, Harold Pinter, Brian Friel, and Tom Stoppard. American writers —

like Edward Albee, John Guare, David Mamet, Maria Fornes — were influenced by him as well. Filmmakers Ingmar Bergman and Woody Allen are among the many who acknowledge Chekhov as their first and foremost influence.

Chekhov's great contribution to dramatic form lies in creating the "bridge" from the classical Western dramatic tradition to the modern era and inviting his successors to cross it. With only four plays, he was able to create that bridge. Bascially, he forged the two classical forms of tragedy and comedy into a form for the modern era — "tragicomedy."

Today, literary historians place Chekhov in the front ranks of world dramatic literature. Ultimately, from Chekhov's point of view, it was not the legacy of his work that concerned him, nor his place in dramatic literature. As he said himself in a letter to Lazarev dated October 20, 1888, "All that I write will be forgotten in five to ten years, but the path paved by me will be free and clear — in this lies my sole merit and contribution."

For Chekhov, the freedom of the writer in his own times to create his own "new forms" is the legacy he wished to leave. This is how he wished to be categorized and remembered. As Treplev says in *The Seagull:* "It's not about forms — old forms, new forms — it's about writing, not bound by any forms at all, just writing, freely, from the soul."

CHEKHOV AND HIS CONTEMPORARIES

"It's a fine thing to be able to remember such a man," remarks Gorky of Chekhov in his *Reminiscences.* "A feeling of joy immediately returns to your life, a clear sense of purpose fills it once more." It is only one of many such appreciations of Chekhov by his numerous friends and acquaintances.

During his lifetime, Chekhov carried on a voluminous correspondence. He wrote over 4,000 letters to family members, fellow writers, publishers, critics, admirers, and friends. These letters cover a variety of topics, including his attitudes toward views on life and literature and his philosophy of writing. He also wrote of his career, his plays, the contemporary theater, and his fellow artists and writers. The quantity of these letters and the wide variety of recipients indicate that Chekhov was basically a gregarious man who loved people (although in later years, as his illness took over, he became more reclusive and ill-humored). He also used his correspondence to express his views on the subject matter that concerned him most — writing and the theater.

This correspondence is also a treasure trove of information on how Chekhov viewed his contemporaries. In turn, his fellow artists and writers wrote memoirs and reminiscences that shed light on Chekhov and how they viewed him.

DOSTOEVSKY AND TURGENEV

Among the great writers who were Chekhov's contemporaries, Dostoevsky had died in 1881, and Turgenev in 1883. Chekhov never met them, as he was only in his early twenties at the time of their deaths, still a medical student, and only a fledgling writer. He had read all their works thoroughly and held them both in awe. He recognized their greatness. However, in later years, he expressed reservations about their writings. He admired Dostoevsky's prodigious oeuvre, but found his novels long and pretentious. Dostoevsky's Slavophilism and religious views were widely divergent from Chekhov's own. As for Turgenev, he admired *A Month in the Country*, whose setting and coterie of characters served as a model for his four major plays. However, he found Turgenev's plays to be lightweight. He didn't admire his female characters, finding them affected and false. Of Turgenev's prose writings, he admired only *Fathers and Sons*. Chekhov became impatient with critics who drew parallels between his work and Turgenev's. "Only a fraction of what he wrote — an eighth to a tenth, say — will last," Chekhov wrote to Olga Knipper on February 13, 1902. "All the rest will be buried in archives in twenty-five to thirty-five years to come."

TOLSTOY AND GORKY

Tolstoy and Gorky (along with Chekhov) were the foremost men of letters of his times. Chekhov developed a close relationship with both. Tolstoy (1828–1910) was the "elder statesman" and father figure, over thirty years Chekhov's senior. While Chekhov did not agree with all of Tolstoy's views (especially his evangelical teachings), he had great admiration for his work and his venerable position in Russian culture. Portraits of Tolstoy and Turgenev graced the walls of his house in Yalta. When he first met Tolstoy in September 1895, he was greatly impressed with his moral authority and his charisma. "He is nearly a perfect man," Chekhov was said to have remarked.

By the time they met face-to-face in 1895, Chekhov had achieved fame as a leading young prose writer of the day, so Tolstoy gave serious consideration to his work. By all reports, Tolstoy admired Chekhov's prose writing but did not care for his plays (with the exception of *The Bear*, which delighted him). Indeed, he made an effort to develop a friendship with Chekhov, to exert a paternal influence on him as a writer, although Chekhov offered a quiet resistance to these attempts. Tolstoy called *The Seagull* weak. He told Nemirovich that *Uncle Vanya* lacked tragic circumstances and that the Art Theatre's production substituted atmosphere and theatrical effect in its place. Moreover, Tolstoy was so outraged by the courtship by Vanya and Astrov of Yelena, a married woman, that he reportedly insulted one of the actors after a performance. He further criticized Chekhov's plays for their trivialities and for having no positive heroes or revolutionaries. (That was precisely the point, Chekhov replied!) Later, according to Troyat, Chekhov remarked, with laughter: "Tolstoy once told me: 'As you know, I detest Shakespeare. And your plays are worse than his.'" The writer Ivan Bunin recalls Chekhov saying: "What I particularly admire in Tolstoy is the contempt he feels for all us writers — not even contempt; he simply considers us all nonexistent."

BASIC BELIEFS

Regarding their basic beliefs, both writers were deeply concerned about the plight of the peasant on the one hand and the lassitude of the intelligentsia on the other. However, Chekhov differed from Tolstoy in two principal regards. Chekhov rejected Tolstoy's belief in Christianity as the main source of moral strength for the Russian peasant. He also rejected the idea of Christianity's ability to cure all evils. As well, Chekhov rejected the methods of social reform advocated by Tolstoy. As a doctor, Chekhov wanted a thorough study of the diseases of society to be made before remedies were suggested. Chekhov considered the ones Tolstoy advocated — like compulsory community programs including physical work for all, and so on — to be superficial and faddish. In turn, according to Bruford, Tolstoy, remarking on the clinical aspects of Chekhov's objective writing, told Gorky that Chekhov would have written better had he not been a doctor.

Despite their differences, however, there was a sincere mutual admiration and an abiding affection of a father/son nature. While in Yalta, they visited on a number of occasions, always memorable to Chekhov. Then in 1900, they were both elected to the Academy of Sciences, which had established a Pushkin Section for Russian Language and Literature. Chekhov and Tolstoy were now considered equal in stature.

In 1903, when Chekhov's health was in decline, Tolstoy tried to cheer him by sending him an inscribed photograph and a list of thirty stories he considered to be Chekhov's finest. (He divided them into two categories of "first" and "second" quality.) He often was known to remark, as Troyat reports: "Chekhov is Pushkin in prose." On other occasions, he compared Chekhov to Maupassant, or to the Impressionist painters. Though Tolstoy lamented that modern Russian writers were not at all Russian in their thought, Chekhov was a glaring exception. "Now you," as Simmons in his biography notes, he once said to Chekhov, "You are Russian. Yes, very very Russian."

CHEKHOV AND GORKY

Chekhov also developed a close relationship with Maxim Gorky (1868–1936). Gorky was a young playwright eight years his junior. As Tolstoy mentored Chekhov, Chekhov in turn mentored Gorky. Their correspondence began with a letter from Gorky to the playwright Chekhov with ecstatic praise for the Art Theatre's production of *The Seagull*. (He was equally enthusiastic about *Uncle Vanya*.) When they met in Yalta in 1899, they struck up a friendship immediately. They spent days discussing art, literature, and politics. It was a relationship of mutual admiration. Chekhov admired Gorky's spontaneity, fierce idealism, and passion for the common man, while Gorky admired Chekhov for his humanity, modesty, and self-effacing qualities. Gorky joined Rachmaninov, Bunin, and Kuprin at the performance of *Uncle Vanya* in Yalta, in honor of the centennial. Chekhov and Gorky so enjoyed each other's company that they traveled together for two weeks that summer of 1900 in the Caucasus. Together, they shared their views of the future of Russia. Gorky, a Marxist, dreamed of revolution; whereas Chekhov hoped for a slower transformation from the czarist regime into enlightened liberalism. Wrote Gorky of his friend: "No one understood so clearly and so shrewdly as Anton Chekhov the tragedy of the trifles of life; no one before him had been able to draw such a mercilessly honest picture of dull, shameful lives . . ."

While both Tolstoy and Gorky were outspoken social activists, it is interesting to note that Chekhov, in his own quiet way, was even more of one. He campaigned against famine, fought epidemics, built schools and public roads in his district around Melikhovo, and endowed libraries. He helped to organize laboratories and gave thousands of peasants free medical treatment. He also planted gardens and trees. He mentored dozens of fledgling writers and helped them find publishers. Meanwhile, he raised funds for human causes and dozens of other pursuits to help his fellow man.

In 1929, the Russian émigré poet Boris Poplavsky commented:

"Dostoevsky cannot help us live, he can only help us when we quarrel, separate, die. Tolstoy perhaps could, but how revolting is his eulogizing of bourgeois prosperity. . . . Chekhov — yes, Chekhov can help us live."

CHEKHOV THE CORRESPONDENT

Chekhov corresponded with dozens of others, including his publishers Nikolai Leikin and Aleksey Suvorin. He wrote to many writers, including Ivan Bunin, Aleksandr Kuprin, Vladimir Korolenko, and Alexey Pleshcheyev. He knew many artists, literary figures, and actors of his day. He was a close friend of the painter Isaak Levitan, and he knew the painter Ilya Repin. He had met the composer Sergei Rachmaninov. He corresponded with the choreographer Sergei Diaghilev and the composer Pyotr Tchaikovsky. He maintained a steady correspondence with Stanislavsky, Nemirovich-Danchenko, and numerous actors at the Moscow Art Theatre. The mutual correspondence between Chekhov and Olga Knipper is a treasure. It includes 400 letters each, approximately, during their courtship and marriage. He also wrote encouraging, supportive letters to numerous young writers who looked to him as a mentor.

In turn, the artists of the day who knew him wrote about him extensively and affectionately in their memoirs. The reminiscences of Ivan Bunin, Aleksandr Kuprin, Nemirovich, Stanislavsky, Olga Knipper, and many others are filled with fond detail of their conversations with Chekhov. They also provide physical descriptions (his smile and other personal characteristics), his jokes, and his profound insights. Above all, they are filled with expressions of respect and admiration for Chekhov as an artist and human being.

In their writings, Chekhov's contemporaries acknowledged him as a writer of the highest order. They placed him in the ranks of Gogol, Dostoevsky, Gonacharov, Turgenev, and Tolstoy. What the critics could not perceive in Chekhov's work, his contemporaries pointed out and admired. They noted the quiet confidence of his voice, the economy of his style, the lack of judgmental tone, the gentle, subversive irony, the breadth and depth of his vision.

His contemporaries recognized he had introduced a new way of thinking and writing in Russia. "The paths I have opened up will remain sound and intact," he said to Gorky. "That is my only value." Bunin, in his reminisces, commented on Chekhov's characteristic self-effacement. "Even though he occupied an eminent place in literature, he was not conscious of his worth." He also remarked, "He was the same with everyone, whatever their status in society." Said Kuprin: "No one could leave him without being overwhelmed by his immense talent and one's own mediocrity."

CHEKHOV'S WORLDVIEW

"You ask: what is life?" writes Chekhov to Olga Knipper not long before his death. "That's exactly like asking: what is a carrot? A carrot is a carrot, and nothing more is known about it." In a nutshell, there we have Chekhov's view of the universe, the world, philosophy, and life.

Chekhov had his finger on the heartbeat of Russia. As a grandson of a serf, a son of a shopkeeper, and an admirer of the gentry, he understood all classes in his culture. As a doctor, he understood people and cared about the quality of their lives. As a social activist, he served mankind. As a Russian, he loved his country, knew its terrain, traveled broadly. As a writer of the *fin de siècle* and the centennial, he felt a responsibility to write about his Russia and his times — like his character Trigorin in *The Seagull*. His vision was broad; his understanding was deep.

Chekhov's plays are seemingly about the landed gentry, set on country estates where people come, people go, and nothing else happens. However, this impression is deceptive. They are the settings on which the story of his times is played out. *Ivanov* presents the tragedy of the "man of the eighties" in Russia. He is an educated, well-intentioned man who realizes that he can do nothing to address the ills, injustices, and hypocrisies of his land and his people and their intransigent way of life. *The Seagull* dramatizes the struggle of the artist and his new voice in a culture where art is stagnant and there is no support for new forms. *Uncle Vanya* dramatizes the tragicomedy of country life, where men and women are trapped by nature and by human nature and can never escape. *The Three Sisters* presents an ensemble of characters at the centennial year in the remote provinces. They are stifled, isolated, guarded by a military troop that cannot defend it against the enemy (backwardness), unable to reach the Moscow that signifies their dreams and their hopes for a future and a better life, unable to see into their future. Finally, *The Cherry Orchard* dramatizes the end — of Russian life as Chekhov knew it, and of Chekhov's own life. His ensemble of endearing, lovable, naïve, flawed characters trapped in a vast land, in an unjust social system, and in their own foibles as human beings cannot change and cannot stave off the inevitable.

Viewing the four major plays as a whole, one can appreciate the breadth and depth of his very special vision. The universality of his themes: love, art, nature (and human nature), death, his passionate love of his country, and his understanding of so many of its aspects, his perception of the passage of time, his subtle sense of history — all contribute to make him a lasting author for our times and those to come. There is also the humanity of his characters: their desires, their weaknesses, their limitations, their dreams and longings, their valiant struggle to love, to endure, to have hope, and to have faith. They want to understand, in the face of all obstacles, "why the cranes fly," as Masha says in *The Three Sisters*. They also experience a desperation to be remembered, somehow, not knowing if they will be.

"MY HOLIEST OF HOLIES . . ."

In a letter to the writer Grigorovich, dated September 10, 1888, the twenty-eight-year-old Chekhov remarked: "I have no philosophy. I change it every month." That is not surprising. Descended from serfs, raised among shopkeepers, he nonetheless admired the nobility for their way of life. On the one hand, he felt great compassion for the peasants and their plight. On the other hand, he hobnobbed with the gentry, the *literati*, and the scientists. On the one hand, he mistrusted religion and the rigid orthodoxy of his parents, which he viewed as hypocritical. On the other hand, he recognized the importance of spirituality in human existence. This was exemplified by characters like Sonya in *Uncle Vanya*.

Chekhov rejected labels and stereotyping. He didn't use Slavophil, Westernizer, liberal, conservative, populist, *narodnik*, Bolshevik, optimist, pessimist. He saw labels as misleading, keeping people from seeing the deeper truths. As he wrote to Suvorin in May 1888: "It's about time that writers admit that you can't figure anything out." Nevertheless, Chekhov did have a prescribed set of values and a consistent view of life. As he says in a letter to Pleshcheyev in October 1888:

> My holiest of holies is the human body, health, intelligence, talent, inspiration, love, and absolute freedom — freedom from violence and freedom from lying, in whatever forms they may take. This is the program I would follow if I were a great artist.

As an artist, he felt his duty was (as expressed in letters to Kiselev and Suvorin) "to be as objective as a chemist" and "not to be the judge of his characters." Rather, he tried to "depict his characters in a true light" and "to pose questions not to answer them." Above all, he championed the notion of freedom — personal, artistic, and spiritual freedom. In a letter to Suvorin, dated January 7, 1889, he wrote:

> Write a story about me: how a young man, the son of a serf, a former shopkeeper, a choir-boy, a school boy, taught to respect rank, to kiss the priests' hands, to worship strange thoughts, to be thankful for his daily bread — a young man who appreciated a frequent beating, went to school without boots, fought with his fists, teased little animals, loved to dine at rich relatives', played the hypocrite before

God and his fellow man only to satisfy his sense of worthlessness — write how this young man is squeezing the slave out of himself, drop by drop, and one morning awakens and feels that slave's blood does not flow in his veins, but real human blood.

CHEKHOV THE HUMANIST

As an adult, Chekhov rejected his father's religion as another kind of labeling. Through his writing, he created his own religion — humanism. His humanism was born of his practice as a doctor, his own abuse as a child, and his steadfast loyalty to his family and friends. It encompassed his capacity for love, compassion, and forgiveness and his sense of humor at his own frailties. This humanism pervades his work. The facets of his humanism were his love of life and his true understanding of its value — of that one lost patient, as Dr. Astrov laments. It also showed his sense of compassion for the human condition and his understanding of human nature and human fallibility. He steadfastly refused to judge his fellow man. He sought to understand him, rather than to condemn him.

While he was aware of the political writings of his day — Marx, Lenin, and so on — Chekhov himself was not a "political writer" *per se*. He did not engage in political polemic in his plays and stories (except in instances like Trofimov in *The Cherry Orchard*). There Chekhov smiles compassionately at a character who believes so blindly in revolutionary propaganda. Instead, humanism was his political affiliation. In his letters, he spoke out against social injustices — such as the inhumane conditions of the penal colony in Sakhalin, or anti-Semitism in the Dreyfus Case in 1898. He also wrote about discrimination against Gorky by the Sciences and Letters after the czar voiced his displeasure about Gorky's reelection. More than specific political points of view, Chekhov was concerned that people live their lives with truth, honesty, and kindness and personal redemption — through work.

Otherwise he kept his eye focused on the big picture — the great sweeping changes that were occurring in his land. The details of everyday life and the foolish preoccupations of the landed gentry that littered his plays were placed there for a reason. They made the backdrop — with its inexorable changes — all the more vivid.

CHEKHOV THE IRONIST

Thus, we perceive the remarkable Janus-like vision that Chekhov had of the century in which he lived and the new century ahead. We see the events he foresaw and did not live to see. In retrospect, knowing what we know now of Russian and world history of our century, the speeches of his characters Astrov, Vershinin, Tusenbach, Lopakhin, and Trofimov haunt us with their prescience.

Ever objective, Chekhov agreed with all his characters. Like Vershinin, he hoped for happiness on earth for generations to come. However, like Tusenbach, he perceived that there are forces in the universe beyond our control. These forces are beyond our grasp and understanding. They determine the future, no matter what we say or do on earth. Like Masha, he still persisted in asking "why," not expecting an answer.

Ultimately, then, there is Chekhov the ironist, who sees the fierce truths of life beyond the efforts of man, beyond history. In these gentle, subtle, evocative plays, he says, like Chebutykin, that "it doesn't matter, it doesn't matter."

This vision and insight was enhanced, in the end, by the fact that Chekhov, from age twenty-eight, knew how short his own life would be. Only a man and a writer like Chekhov could have recognized this mortal fact as a gift with which to enrich his art so that others might benefit.

DRAMATIC MOMENTS

from the Major Plays

These short excerpts are from the playwright's major plays. They give a taste of the work of the play-wright. Each has a short introduction that helps the reader understand the context of the excerpt. The excerpts illustrate the main themes mentioned in the In an Hour essay and are in chronological order.

from **The Seagull**

CHARACTERS

Treplev
Nina
Dorn
Arkadina
Polina Andreevna
Yakov
Masha
Shamraev
Trigorin

[In this final scene of the play and Act Four, the young writer Treplev is visited by the actress Nina, whom he has loved for years. She has forsaken him for an affair with Trigorin, who is another writer as well as Treplev's mother's lover. Nina has been deeply wounded by Trigorin's abandonment, and she finds that her only opportunity to work can be found in second-rate provincial theaters.

Still, she is determined to survive as an actress. Treplev, however, finds that his spirit as a writer has been broken by unrequited love and loss of inspiration. The two young theater artists have paid too great a price for their art.]

TREPLEV: (*Preparing to write, reviews what he has already written.*) Forms. For so long I've been going on and on about the need for new forms. And now, little by little, I'm falling into the same old rut myself. (*Reads.*) "The poster on the fence proclaimed it . . . a pale face, framed by dark hair" . . . "proclaimed," "framed" . . . It's so trite. (*Crosses it out.*) I'll start with the part where the hero is awakened by the sound of the rain, and strike all the rest. All this about a moonlit night is drawn-out and pretentious. Now Trigorin has technique, it's easy for him . . . He's got a "broken bottle neck gleaming on the bank," a "mill wheel casting a somber shadow" — and presto — there's his moonlit night right there. And what do I have — "the shimmering light," and "the soft twinkling of the stars," and "the distant sounds of the piano receding into the quiet, fragrant air" . . . I mean, it's unbearable!

Pause.

Yes, more and more I've come to see . . . it's not about forms — old forms, new forms — it's about writing, not bound by any forms at all, just writing, freely, from the soul.

Someone raps on the window near the writing table.

What's that? *(Looks out the window.)* I can't see anything . . . *(Opens the glass door and looks out into the garden.)* Someone's running down the steps. *(Calls out.)* Who's there? *(Exits; he can be heard walking rapidly along the terrace; a moment later, he returns with NINA.)* Nina! Nina!

Nina lays her head on his chest and sobs with restraint.

(Deeply moved.) Nina! Nina! It's you . . . it's you . . . I knew it — all day long my soul has been in anguish. *(Takes off her hat and cape.)* Oh, my darling, my beloved — she's come! Let's not cry, please, let's not!

NINA: Someone's here.

TREPLEV: No, no one.

NINA: Lock the doors, someone will come in.

TREPLEV: No one will come in.

NINA: Irina Nikolaevna is here, I know it. Please lock the doors . . .

TREPLEV: *(Locks the right door with a key, and then crosses to the left.)* There's no lock on this one. I'll put a chair against it. *(Puts armchair against the door.)* Don't worry, no one will come in.

NINA: *(Gazes at him intently.)* Let me look at you. *(Looks around.)* It's so warm in here, so lovely . . . This used to be the living room. Have I changed a lot?

TREPLEV: Yes ... You're thinner, and your eyes are bigger, much bigger. Nina, it's so strange to be seeing you. Why didn't you ever let me visit you? Why didn't you come sooner? I know you've been here almost a week already ... Every day I've been coming over, time and time again, I stand outside your window like a beggar.

NINA: I was afraid you'd hate me. Every night I have the same dream — you look at me and you don't recognize me. If only you knew! From the moment I arrived I've been coming here ... to walk by the lake. I've gone past your house so many times, but I couldn't bring myself to come in. Come, let's sit down.

They sit.

Let's just sit and talk. It's so lovely here, isn't it, so warm, so safe ... Oh! Do you hear it? The wind? There's a line in Turgenev that goes: "Lucky is he who, on nights like these, has a roof over his head, a warm place to sit." I'm a seagull ... No, that's not it. (*Rubs her forehead.*) What was I saying? Oh, yes ... Turgenev ... "And God watches over all homeless wanderers ..." Never mind. (*Sobs.*)

TREPLEV: Nina, not again ... Nina!

NINA: Never mind, really, it feels much better, it does ... I haven't cried in two years. Late last night, I went out in the garden, to see if our theatre were still there. And it is — it's there, it's been there all this time! I burst out crying for the first time in two years, and a weight, such a weight lifted from my soul. You see, I'm not crying any more! (*Takes his hand.*) So, you've become a writer after all ... You're a writer, and I'm an actress ... We're drawn into the vortex, both of us ... I used to be so happy, blissful, like a child — I'd wake up every morning and burst out singing. I loved you, I dreamed of fame ... and now? Tomorrow morning early it's off to Yelets, third class ... with the peasants, and then in Yelets, it's the businessmen, with their little "invitations." What a miserable life!

TREPLEV: Why Yelets?

NINA: I've taken an engagement there for the winter season. It's time for me to go.

TREPLEV: Nina. I've cursed you, hated you, torn your letters and photographs to pieces, but every minute I knew my soul was bound to you forever. To stop loving you is not within my power, Nina. From the moment I lost you, and after that, even when my work started to be published, my life has been unbearable — I suffer so much . . . It's as if my youth had suddenly been stripped away from me, and I feel I've been living endless years upon this earth. I call out your name, I kiss the ground you walk on — wherever I look, I see your face before me, your tender smile, that smile which illuminated the most precious years of my life . . .

NINA: *(Dismayed.)* Why are you talking like this, why?

TREPLEV: I'm alone, with no love to warm me, I'm cold, it's like living in a grave, and no matter what I write, no matter what, it's flat, stale, lifeless. Stay here, Nina, I beg of you, or else let me go away with you.

NINA quickly puts on her hat and cape.

Nina, why? For God's sake, Nina . . . *(Watches her put her things on.)*

Pause.

NINA: My horses are waiting at the gate. Don't bother to come out, I can find my own way . . . *(In tears.)* Give me some water.

TREPLEV: *(Gives her water.)* Where are you going now?

NINA: Into town.

Pause.

Is Irina Nikolaevna here?

TREPLEV: Yes . . . Thursday, my uncle took ill. We cabled her to come.

NINA: Why do you say you kiss the ground I walk on? I ought to be killed. *(Leans against the table.)* I'm so exhausted. If only I could rest, just rest. *(Lifts her head.)* I'm a seagull! . . . No, that's not it. I'm an actress. Yes, that's right! *(She hears ARKADINA and TRIGORIN's laughter, listens, then runs to the left door and looks through the keyhole.)* So, he is here, too . . . *(Turns to TREPLEV.)* Ah well . . . what does it matter . . . Yes . . . He never believed in the theatre, you know, he always laughed at my dreams, and little by little I stopped believing and lost faith, too . . . And then there were the pressures of love, the jealousy, the constant worry over my little one . . . I became — I don't know — mediocre, pitiful, my acting made no sense any more . . . I didn't know what to do with my hands, how to stand on stage, how to control my own voice. You have no idea how it feels, to know you're acting badly. I'm a seagull. No that's not it . . . Do you remember, when you shot that seagull? "One day, by chance, there came a man who saw her and, for lack of anything better to do, destroyed her" . . . An idea for a short story . . . No, that's not it . . . *(Rubs her forehead.)* What was I saying? . . . Oh yes, I was talking about the stage. No, I'm not like that any more . . . I'm a true actress now, and I perform with joy, with ecstasy, I'm intoxicated on the stage, and I feel beautiful. And now, while I've been staying here, I've been walking, walking and thinking, thinking and feeling, how my spirit is growing stronger every day . . . And now I know, I understand, Kostya, that in our work — it's all the same, whether we perform or we write — the main thing is not the glory, not the glitter, no, not any of those things I dreamed of, it's having the strength to endure. The strength to bear your cross, to have faith. I have faith, and it's not so painful for me any more, and when I think about my calling, I'm not so afraid of life. I'm not.

TREPLEV: *(Sadly.)* You've found your way, you know where you're going, while I'm still floundering in a sea of dreams and images, not knowing what or whom they are for. I don't believe in anything, and I don't know what my calling is.

NINA: *(Listening.)* Shh . . . I'm going. Good-bye. When I become a famous actress, come and see me. Promise? But now . . . *(Squeezes his hand.)* It's late — I can hardly stand . . . I'm so exhausted, so hungry . . .

TREPLEV: Stay, let me give you some supper . . .

NINA: No, no . . . don't bother, I'll find my way out . . . My horses are near . . . So, she brought him with her. Well, what does it matter. When you see Trigorin, tell him nothing . . . I love him. I love him even more than ever . . . An idea for a short story . . . I love him, I love him passionately, I love him to distraction. How glorious it was then, wasn't it, Kostya! Do you remember? What a life! A clear, warm, joyful, pure life, and what feelings — feelings like delicate, lovely flowers . . . Do you remember? . . . *(Recites.)* "Men, lions, eagles and partridges, horned stags, geese, spiders, the silent fish dwelling deep in the waters, starfish, and creatures invisible to the naked eye — all life, all life, all life, its sad cycle ended, has died away. Thousands of centuries have passed since the earth has borne any living creature, and the poor moon in vain lights up her lantern. No longer do the waking cranes cry out in the meadow, and maybugs are silent in the lime groves."

Embraces TREPLEV impetuously and runs out through the glass door.

TREPLEV: *(After a pause.)* I hope no one sees her in the garden and tells Mama. It might upset Mama . . . *(For the next two minutes, in silence, he tears up all his manuscripts and throws them under the writing table; then he unlocks the right door and exits.)*

DORN: *(Trying to open the door stage left.)* That's strange . . . The door's locked, somehow . . . *(Enters and puts the armchair in its place.)* It's like an obstacle course in here.

Enter ARKADINA, POLINA ANDREEVNA, behind them, YAKOV carrying bottles, and MASHA, then SHAMRAEV and TRIGORIN.

ARKADINA: Put the red wine and the beer for Boris Alekseevich here on the table. We'll have something to drink while we're playing. Let's be seated, everyone.

POLINA ANDREEVNA: *(To YAKOV.)* And bring the tea in, right away. *(Lights the candles, sits at the card table.)*

SHAMRAEV: *(Takes TRIGORIN over to the cupboard.)* Here's the thing I was talking about just now . . . *(Takes a mounted seagull out of the cupboard.)* As requested.

TRIGORIN: *(Looks at the seagull.)* I don't remember! *(Thinks for a moment.)* I don't remember!

To the right, offstage, a shot; all are startled.

ARKADINA: *(Frightened.)* What was that?

DORN: Nothing, something exploded in my medicine bag, most likely. Don't worry. *(He exits through the door stage right, and after a few moments, returns.)* That was it. A bottle of ether exploded. *(Hums.)* "Again, before you I stand, enchanted . . . "

ARKADINA: *(Sitting at the table.)* Oh, I was so frightened. It reminded me of the time . . . *(Covers her face with her hands.)* For a moment, everything went dark . . .

DORN: *(Looking through a magazine, to TRIGORIN.)* Two months ago an article was published here . . . a letter from America, and I wanted to ask you, by the way . . . *(Puts an arm around TRIGORIN and leads him downstage.)* since I was so interested in this issue . . . *(In a low voice, under his breath.)* Get Irina Nikolaevna out of here. The fact is, Konstantin Gavrilovich has just shot himself . . .

CURTAIN

from **Uncle Vanya**

CHARACTERS

Marina
Astrov
Ivan Voynitsky (Vanya)
Serebryakov
Yelena Andreevna
Telegin
Sonya
Maria Vasilyevna

[In this opening scene of Act One, we meet the characters of Chekhov's second major play, whose lives will be entangled in a summer of love intrigue and family confrontation. In the speeches of Astrov, the lonely country doctor, and his friend Ivan Voynitsky (Vanya), a frustrated intellectual whose life has been wasted running the family estate and serving his scholarly brother-in-law, we learn of the isolation and hopelessness of country life.]

The garden. Part of the house and terrace are visible. On the pathway, under an old poplar tree, is a table, set for tea. There are benches and chairs; on one of the benches lies a guitar. Not far from the table, there is a swing. It is between two and three o'clock in the afternoon and overcast.

MARINA, a plump, slow-moving little old lady, sits by the samovar, knitting a stocking, and ASTROV paces nearby.

MARINA: *(Pours a glass of tea.)* Drink up, dearie.
ASTROV: *(Reluctantly takes the glass.)* I don't feel like it.
MARINA: How about a little vodka, then?
ASTROV: No. I don't drink vodka every day. Anyway, it's too hot.

Pause.

So, nanny, how far back do we go, you and I?

MARINA: *(Reflecting.)* How far back? Lord, let me think . . . you came out here to our part of the world . . . when was it? . . . Vera Petrovna was still alive, Sonechkina's mother. Her last two winters you came to us . . . remember? So, let me see, that must be, what, eleven years ago. *(After a moment.)* Or even more, maybe, who knows . . .

ASTROV: Have I changed a lot since that time?

MARINA: Yes, a lot. You were young then, young and handsome . . . And now, you've gotten old. And you're not so good-looking any more. All that vodka, it doesn't help, you know.

ASTROV: Yes . . . Ten years, and I've become someone else. And why? I'm overworked, nanny. On my feet from morning till night, not a moment's peace, and then in bed at night I lie under the covers, terrified that they're coming to drag me out on a call. In all the time I've known you, not a single day of rest, not one. How could I not age? Tell me. Yes, this life is boring, stupid, squalid . . . And it drags you down, this life, it does. You live, surrounded by strange people, no, really, each and every one of them, truly strange; and two or three years go by, and little by little, without knowing it, you've become strange yourself! It's inevitable! *(Fiddles with his moustache.)* Look at this huge moustache I've grown . . . ridiculous, isn't it! I've become an eccentric, nanny . . . I mean, thank God, I'm not stupid yet, no, that I'm not, my brain's still intact, but my feelings have grown numb, somehow . . . I want nothing, need nothing, love no one . . . Except you, nanny, you I love. *(Kisses the top of her head.)* I had a nanny once, just like you.

MARINA: Perhaps you'd like something to eat?

ASTROV: No. Third week of Lent, I went to Malitskoe for the epidemic . . . Typhus . . . In the huts, on the floor, wall-to-wall bodies . . . Mud, stench, filth . . . calves on the floor, lying right there, alongside the sick . . . Pigs, too . . . I worked all day long, never sat down, never ate a morsel of food, and no sooner do I get home, not a moment's rest — they bring the switchman over from the railroad yard;

I lay him out on the table, you know, for surgery, and he up and dies on me under chloroform. Just like that. Right on the spot. And that's when my feelings come alive again, just when I don't need them . . . and my conscience starts to torment me, as if I'd killed him myself, on purpose . . . I sat down, right then and there, I closed my eyes — just like this, and I thought: those who will live after us, one hundred – two hundred years from now, those for whom we show the way, will they remember us kindly? Will they? No, nanny, they won't!

MARINA: People won't, but God will.

ASTROV: Thanks, nanny. Well said.

VOYNITSKY (VANYA) enters.

VANYA: *(Enters from the house; he has had a nap after lunch and looks rumpled; sits on the bench and adjusts his dapper tie.)*
Yes . . .

Pause.

Yes . . .

ASTROV: Had a good nap?

VANYA: Yes . . . Very. *(Yawns.)* Since the advent of our professor and his blushing bride, life has been complete chaos . . . I sleep at the wrong time, eat all kinds of rich nonsense for lunch and dinner, drink wine . . . unhealthy, that's what it is! Before, there was not a moment to spare, how Sonya and I would work, bless our hearts, and now, Sonya toils away all alone, while I sleep, eat, drink . . . it's not right!

MARINA: *(Shakes her head.)* It's the new way! The professor gets up at eleven, and meanwhile the samovar's been boiling all morning, everybody's waiting for him. Before they came, we used to have our midday meal at one, like normal people, and now we eat at seven. Then the professor's up all night reading and writing, and suddenly at two in the morning the bell rings . . . What in the world . . . ? Tea, he wants! And it's "Wake up everybody, get the samovar started" . . . The new way!

ASTROV: And how long will they be staying?

VANYA: *(Whistles.)* One hundred years. The professor has decided to settle here for good.

MARINA: And that's how it is nowadays. The samovar's been going for two hours already, and they went for a walk.

VANYA: They're coming, they're coming . . . Don't get upset.

Voices are heard; SEREBRYAKOV, YELENA ANDREEVNA, SONYA, and TELEGIN enter from the garden, returning from their walk.

SEREBRYAKOV: Splendid, splendid . . . Glorious views.

TELEGIN: Remarkable, your excellency.

SONYA: And tomorrow, we'll take a walk in the forests, Papa. All right?

VANYA: Ladies and gentlemen, tea is served!

SEREBRYAKOV: My dear friends, be so kind as to bring the tea to my study, would you? I still have some catching up to do today.

SONYA: You'll love the forests, I know you will . . .

YELENA ANDREEVNA, SEREBRYAKOV, and SONYA go into the house; TELEGIN goes to the table and sits down next to MARINA.

VANYA: It's hot out, it's stifling, and our esteemed scholar sports an overcoat and galoshes, complete with umbrella and gloves.

ASTROV: Takes care of himself, doesn't he?

VANYA: And how marvelous she is! Simply marvelous! I've never seen a more beautiful woman in my entire life.

TELEGIN: When I drive through the field, Marina Timofeevna, when I walk through the shady garden, when I look at this tea table, I experience such indescribable bliss! The weather is lovely, the little birds sing, we live in peace and harmony, — what more could we want? *(Takes a glass.)* I'm deeply grateful to you.

VANYA: *(Dreamily.)* Those eyes . . . A magnificent woman.

ASTROV: So tell me something, Ivan Petrovich.

VANYA: *(Listlessly.)* What's there to tell?

ASTROV: Anything new, at least?

VANYA: Nothing's new. It's all old. I'm the same as I was, thank you very much, only worse, I've gotten lazy, I don't do a thing, except grumble, like an old goat. My dear 'Maman,' the old crow, still babbles on and on all the time about women's emancipation; she's got one foot in the grave, and the other in her beloved library, searching for the dawn of a new life.

ASTROV: And the professor?

VANYA: And the professor, as always, from dawn till deepest night, sits in his study and writes. And writes.

> "With strained mind, with furrowed brow,
>   Our sacred odes we write,
>   Yet hear we not a word of praise,
>   Although we wish we might."

The poor, poor paper! Better he should write his autobiography! Now what a sublime subject that would be! A retired professor, listen to this, a dried up old stick, a scholarly old trout . . . Rheumatism, gout, migraines, liver jaundiced with jealousy and envy . . . Lives on the estate of his first wife, this old trout does, lives here against his will, mind you, because living in town is far more than he can possibly afford. Forever complains about his misfortunes, although, truth be told, he is a very very fortunate man, oh yes, abnormally so. *(Irritably.)* You can't imagine how fortunate! The son of a simple sexton, a seminarian, and he goes and gets himself a doctoral degree, a faculty chair, a title of your excellency, a senator for a father-in-law, and so on, and so on, and so on, blah, blah, blah. But never mind, forget about all that. Now, here comes the good part. This is a man who for twenty-five years precisely has been reading and writing about art, while understanding absolutely nothing about art. For twenty-five years he regurgitates someone else's theories on realism, naturalism, and all other kinds of ridiculous nonsense; for twenty-five years he reads and writes about things that intelligent people have already known for a long, long time, and stupid people find boring anyway; in other words, for twenty-five years he's been pouring from one empty vessel into another. And all the while behold, what self-importance! What grandiosity! He is retired, and not one living, breathing soul has ever even heard of him, he's an utter unknown; in other words, for twenty-five years he's been occupying someone else's place. Yet, behold: how he parades around, like a demi-god!

ASTROV: Sounds like you're jealous.

VANYA: Of course, I'm jealous! And what success with women! Don Juan himself never knew such success! His first wife, my sister, a lovely, gentle creature, pure as that blue sky up above, noble, warm-hearted, with far more admirers than he ever had students, — loved him as only the purest of angels above can love others as pure and perfect as themselves. My mother, his mother-in-law, worships him till this day, till this very day he inspires in her a kind of religious awe. His second wife, a beauty, a fine woman — you just saw her, — married him when he was already an old man, gave up her youth for him, her beauty, her freedom, her radiance. What for? Why? Tell me.

ASTROV: Is she faithful to the professor?

VANYA: Unfortunately, yes.

ASTROV: Why unfortunately?

VANYA: Because this fidelity is false from start to finish. It has rhyme, but no reason. To be unfaithful to an old husband whom you can't stand any more — that's immoral; to suffocate the youth and vitality living and breathing inside you — that's not?

TELEGIN: *(Whining.)* Vanya, I don't like it, when you talk that way. Now, really . . . He who betrays his wife, or husband, he is an unfaithful soul, one who is capable of betraying his own country.

VANYA: *(Annoyed.)* Oh dry up, Waffles!

TELEGIN: Permit me to continue, Vanya. My own wife ran away from me the day after our wedding with her lover, because of my unattractive appearance. Yet since that time I have never broken my vow to her. I have loved her to this very day and have remained faithful to her, I've helped her however I can, I've even given up my own property for the education of the children she brought into this world with her lover. My happiness I have lost, but I've kept my pride. And she? Her youth has long since gone, her beauty has faded according to nature's laws, her lover has died . . . What does she have left?

Enter SONYA and YELENA ANDREEVNA; a moment later, enter MARIA VASILYEVNA with a book; she sits and reads; tea is served to her, and she drinks, oblivious.

CURTAIN

from **The Three Sisters**

CHARACTERS

Masha
Kulygin
Irina
Olga
Natasha
Andrey
Ferapont
Vershinin

[In the third act of Chekhov's third major play, while a fire rages in the provincial town around them, the three Prozorov sisters see all their dreams — of going to Moscow and finding love and fulfillment — burning down around them, too.]

MASHA: You ought to go home.

KULYGIN: My darling Masha, my precious Masha . . .

IRINA: She's exhausted. Let her rest, Fedya.

KULYGIN: I'm going, right away . . . My wife, she's so lovable, so adorable . . . I love you, my only one . . .

MASHA: "Amo, amas, amat, amamus, amatis, amant."

KULYGIN: *(Laughs.)* No, really, she's wonderful. I've been married to you for seven years, and yet it seems we were married only yesterday. Word of honor. No, really, you're a wonderful woman. I'm content, I'm content, I'm content!

MASHA: I'm miserable, miserable, miserable . . . *(Sits up and speaks.)* And I can't get it out of my head . . . It's simply disgraceful. It's like a nail boring into my brain, I can't keep silent. I'm talking about Andrey . . . He's mortgaged this house to the bank, and his wife has appropriated all the money, but this house doesn't belong to him alone, it belongs to all four of us! Surely, he must know that, if he were in the least bit honorable, that is.

KULYGIN: Must you, Masha? What's the point? Andryusha owes money to everyone, God bless him.

MASHA: Whatever, it's disgraceful. *(Lies down.)*

KULYGIN: We're not poor, you and I. I work, I go to the high school, I give lessons . . . I'm an honest man. A simple man . . . "Omnia mea mecum porto," as they say.

MASHA: I don't need anything, it's just that I can't bear the injustice, it enrages me.

Pause.

Go home, Fyodor!

KULYGIN: *(Kisses her.)* You're tired, rest for half an hour, I'll sit up and wait for you. Sleep . . . *(Exiting.)* I'm content, I'm content, I'm content. *(Exits.)*

IRINA: No, really, how our Andrey's aged, how he's weakened, how he's wasted away, living with that woman. Once, he was going to become a professor, and now, only yesterday, he's boasting that he's finally been appointed to the local district council. Andrey, a member of the local district council, whose chairman is Protopopov . . . The whole town is talking about him, laughing at him, and he alone doesn't know it and doesn't see it . . . Look, how everyone runs to the fire, and he sits in his room, oblivious to it all. Playing his violin. *(Upset.)* Oh, how awful it is, how awful, how awful! *(Weeps.)* I can't bear it any longer, I can't! . . . I can't, I can't! . . .

Enter OLGA, she tidies the area near her table.

(Sobs loudly.) Throw me out, throw me out, I can't bear it any longer!

OLGA: *(Frightened.)* What is it, what is it? Darling!

IRINA: *(Sobbing.)* Where? Where has it all gone to? Where? Oh my God, my God! I've forgotten everything, everything . . . It's all muddled up in my head . . . I can't remember the word in Italian for "window," or "ceiling" . . . I've forgotten everything. Every day I keep forgetting, and life is passing by us, never to return, never, we'll never go to Moscow . . . I see it now, we'll never go, ever . . .

OLGA: Darling, darling . . .

IRINA: *(Containing herself.)* Oh, how unhappy I am . . . I can't work, I can't bear to work. It's enough, enough! I worked in the telegraph office, now I work for the town council and I hate, no, I despise everything they give me to do . . . I'm almost twenty-four years old, I've been working forever, and my brain has shrivelled up, I've grown old, and thin, and ugly, and nothing, nothing gives me any satisfaction whatsoever, and meanwhile time passes by, and it's almost as if we're disappearing, fading away from all hope of a truly beautiful life, fading further and further away into some kind of abyss. I despair, and why I'm alive, why I haven't killed myself by now, I don't understand.

OLGA: Don't cry, my child, don't cry . . . I suffer so.

IRINA: I won't cry, I won't . . . Enough . . . There, you see, I'm not crying any more. Enough . . . Enough!

OLGA: Darling, I'm speaking to you as a sister, as a friend, if you want my advice, marry the baron!

IRINA weeps softly.

You respect him, you do, you admire him . . . He's not handsome, it's true, but he's so decent, so pure . . . We don't marry for love, really we don't, we marry for duty. That's what I think, at least, and I'd marry without love, I would. Whoever proposed to me, it wouldn't matter, I'd marry him, as long as he were decent. I'd even marry an old man . . .

IRINA: I've waited forever, to move to Moscow, to meet my own true love, I've dreamed of him, loved him . . . But it's all turned out to be such nonsense, such nonsense . . .

OLGA: *(Embraces her sister.)* My darling, my beautiful sister, I understand everything; when Baron Nikolai Lvovich left the military service and came to visit in civilian clothes, he looked so homely, I burst into tears . . . "Why are you crying?" he asked. How could I tell him! But if it's God's will that you marry him, then that would make me happy. That, you see, is different, altogether different.

NATASHA crosses silently from the door stage right to the door stage left, carrying a candle.

MASHA: *(Sits.)* She walks around here as if she started the fire herself.
OLGA: Masha, you're silly. You're the silliest one in the family. Forgive me, please . . .

Pause.

MASHA: I have something to confess, darling sisters, My soul is in anguish. I shall confess it to you and you alone, and never again to anyone, anywhere . . . And I shall tell it to you now. *(Softly.)* It is my secret, but you should know everything . . . I cannot keep silent . . .

Pause.

I love, I love . . . I love this man . . . You've only just seen him. There, now you know. I love Vershinin . . .
OLGA: *(Goes behind her screen partition.)* Stop it. It doesn't matter, I'm not listening.
MASHA: What can I do! *(Holds her head in her hands.)* At first, I thought him strange, then I pitied him . . . then I fell in love with him . . . I fell in love with his voice, his words, his misfortunes, his two little girls . . .
OLGA: *(From behind the screen.)* It doesn't matter, I'm not listening. Whatever foolish things you're saying, it doesn't matter, I'm not listening.
MASHA: You're the foolish one, Olya. I love him — that, you see, is my

fate. That is my lot in life, you see . . . And he loves me . . . It's all so awful. Isn't it? Isn't it terrible? *(Takes IRINA by the hand, draws her close.)* Oh my darling . . . Somehow we shall live through life, whatever it has in store for us . . . You know, when you're reading some novel or other, and everything seems so predictable, so obvious, and then you fall in love yourself, then, only then do you see, that no one knows anything, and each of us must find her own way . . . My darlings, my sisters . . . There, I've confessed to you, and now I shall be silent . . . Like Gogol's madman . . . silence . . . silence . . .

Enter ANDREY, followed by FERAPONT.

ANDREY: *(Angrily.)* What do you want? I don't understand.

FERAPONT: *(At the door, impatiently.)* But, Andrey Sergeevich, I've already told you ten times.

ANDREY: First of all, it's not Andrey Sergeevich, it's "Your honor."

FERAPONT: It's about the firemen, your honor, they're asking permission to pass through the garden to get to the river. Otherwise they'll have to go all the way 'round the house, 'round and 'round. And that, well, that's a big problem.

ANDREY: All right. Tell them it's all right.

FERAPONT exits.

I'm sick of all this. Where's Olga?

OLGA appears from behind the screen.

I've come to ask you for the key to the wardrobe, I've lost mine. You've got a little key, haven't you?

OLGA gives him the key, silently. IRINA goes behind her screen partition. Pause.

What an enormous fire! It's dying down, now. That Ferapont, damn it, he gets on my nerves, and then I say the stupidest things to him . . . "Your honor" . . .

Pause.

Why are you so quiet, Olya?

Pause.

It's time to stop all this foolishness and resentment, there's no reason for it. You're here, Masha, Irina's here, so, well, good — let's have it all out, once and for all. What do you have against me? What?

OLGA: Stop it, Andryusha. We'll talk it over tomorrow. *(Upset.)* What a cruel night!

ANDREY: *(Very flustered.)* Don't get upset. I'm completely calm and collected, and I'm asking you: What do you have against me? Tell me the truth.

VERSHININ's voice: "Tram-tam-tam!"

MASHA: *(Stands, loudly.)* Tra-ta-ta! *(To OLGA.)* Good-bye, Olya, God bless you. *(She goes behind the curtain, kisses IRINA.)* Sleep well . . . Good-bye, Andrey. Go, they're all worn out . . . we'll talk it over tomorrow . . . *(Exits.)*

OLGA: Really, Andryusha, let's leave it till tomorrow . . . *(Goes behind her screen partition.)* It's time for sleep.

ANDREY: Just let me say it, then I'll go. All right . . . First of all, you have something against Natasha, my wife, this I have known from the day of my wedding. Natasha is a fine, decent person, honest, and honorable — that is my opinion. She is my wife, I love and respect her, do you understand, I respect her, and I demand that others respect her as well. I repeat, she is an honest, honorable person, and your disapproval, forgive me, is simply an indulgence.

Pause.

Second, you're angry with me, apparently, that I'm not a professor, that I didn't become a scientist. But I serve the district, I am a member of the local district council, that is my service, and I consider it to be as sacred and as noble as the service to science. I am a member of the local district council, and proud of it, if you really want to know . . .

Pause.

Third . . . I still have more to say . . . I have mortgaged the house, without asking your permission . . . I am guilty of this, yes, and I ask your forgiveness. My debts drove me to it . . . Thirty-five thousand . . . I no longer play cards, that I gave up a long time ago, but the main thing, and may I say this in my own defense, is that you girls, you all receive a pension, whereas I've had no . . . income myself, so to speak . . .

Pause.

KULYGIN: *(In the doorway.)* Masha's not here? *(Anxiously.)* Where is she, then? That's strange . . . *(Exits.)*

ANDREY: They aren't listening. Natasha is a outstanding person, a person of the highest integrity. *(He roams about the stage in silence, then stops.)* When I married her, I thought we'd be happy . . . so very happy . . . But my God . . . *(Weeps.)* My dearest sisters, my darling sisters, don't believe me, don't believe me . . . *(Exits.)*

KULYGIN: *(In the doorway, anxiously.)* Where's Masha? Masha's not here? That's surprising. *(Exits.)*

The alarm bell sounds, the stage is empty.

IRINA: *(From behind the screen.)* Olya! Who is knocking on the floor?
OLGA: It's the doctor, Ivan Romanich. He's drunk.
IRINA: What a bewildering night!

Pause.

Olya! *(Peers out from behind the screen.)* Did you hear? They're taking the brigade from us, they're moving it somewhere far far away.

OLGA: It's only a rumor.

IRINA: And then we shall be left alone . . . Olya!

OLGA: What?

IRINA: Dearest, darling, I respect the baron, I admire him, I do, he's a fine person, I'll marry him, I'll agree to it, only then let us go to Moscow! I beg of you, let us go! There is no place else on earth for us but Moscow! Let's go, Olya! Let's go!

CURTAIN

from **The Cherry Orchard**

CHARACTERS

Varya
Lyubov Andeevna
Trofimov
Gaev
Lopakhin
Yepikhodov
Anya
Firs
Passerby

[In the second act of Chekhov's final play, we see the residents of a family estate, where time is standing still, captured in a moment of Russian history (the turn of the twentieth century). The past (and their way of life) is slipping away, the present teeters on a precipice of tumultuous change, and the future lies uncharted before them.]

VARYA: Petya, you do better when you talk about astronomy.

LYUBOV ANDREEVNA: No, let's continue yesterday's conversation.

TROFIMOV: What about?

GAEV: About pride. Pride in man.

TROFIMOV: That. We talked about that forever, but we did not come to any conclusion. According to your way of thinking, there is something mystical about the proud man, an aura, almost. Perhaps you are correct in your beliefs, but if you analyze the issue clearly, without complicating things, then why does this pride even exist, what reason can there be for pride, if a man is not physically distinguished, if the vast majority of mankind is coarse, stupid, or profoundly miserable. There is no time for the admiration of self. There is only time for work.

GAEV: We're all going to die, anyway, so what difference does it make?

TROFIMOV: Who knows? And what does it really mean — to die? For all we know, man is endowed with a hundred sensibilities, and when he dies, only the five known to us perish along with him, while the other ninety-five remain alive.

LYUBOV ANDREEVNA: How intelligent you are, Petya! . . .

LOPAKHIN: *(Ironically.)* Yes, terribly!

TROFIMOV: Mankind marches onward, ever onward, strengthening his skills, his capacities. All that has up until now been beyond his reach may one day be attainable, only he must work, indeed, he must do everything in his power to help those who seek the truth. In Russia, however, very few people actually do work. The vast majority of the intelligentsia, as I know them, do nothing, pursue nothing, and, meanwhile, have no predisposition whatsoever to work, they're completely incapable of it. They call themselves 'the intelligentsia,' and yet they address their servants with disrespect, they treat the peasants as if they were animals, they're dismal students, they're poorly educated, they never read serious literature, they're absolutely idle, they don't do a thing except sit around talking about science and art, about which they know nothing at all. And they're all so grim looking, they have tense, taut faces, they only talk about 'important things,' they spend all their time philosophizing, and meanwhile, right before their very eyes, the workers live atrociously, eat abominably, sleep without bedding, thirty-forty to a room, together with bedbugs, stench, dankness, depravity . . . And so it seems that all this lofty talk is simply meant to conceal the truth from themselves and others. Show me, please, where are the day nurseries, about which they speak so much and so often, where are the public reading rooms? They only write about them in novels, they never become a reality, never. There is only filth, vulgarity, barbarism . . . I dread their serious countenances, their serious conversations, I despise them. Better to be silent!

LOPAKHIN: You know, I get up before five every morning, I work from dawn until night, I deal with money, constantly, mine and others, and yes, I see how people really are. You only have to try to get something done to realize how few honest, decent people there are in this world. Sometimes, when I can't fall asleep, I lie there thinking: "Dear Lord, you have given us the vast forests, the boundless plains, the endless horizons, and we who live here on this earth, we should be true giants . . . "

LYUBOV ANDREEVNA: What good are giants . . . They're very nice in fairy tales, you know, but in true life, they're terrifying.

YEPIKHODOV crosses upstage, playing the guitar.

(Pensively.) There goes Yepikhodov.

ANYA: *(Pensively.)* There goes Yepikhodov.
GAEV: The sun has set, ladies and gentlemen.
TROFIMOV: Yes.
GAEV: *(Softly, as if reciting.)* O nature, wondrous nature, you shine on, radiant and eternal, beauteous and indifferent, you whom we call mother, you embody birth and death, you create and you destroy, you . . .
VARYA: *(Imploring.)* Uncle, dear!
ANYA: Not again, Uncle!
TROFIMOV: You're better off "pocketing the yellow . . . "
GAEV: I'll be quiet, I'll be quiet.

All sit, deep in thought. Silence. Only FIRS's muttering can be heard. Suddenly from far, far away, a sound is heard, as if coming from the sky, the sound of a breaking string, dying away in the distance, a mournful sound.

LYUBOV ANDREEVNA: What was that?
LOPAKHIN: Don't know. Somewhere far away, deep in the mines, a bucket broke loose and fell . . . But somewhere very far away.

GAEV: Or a bird of some kind . . . a heron, perhaps.

TROFIMOV: Or an owl . . .

LYUBOV ANDREEVNA: *(Shudders.)* Disturbing, somehow.

Pause.

FIRS: Right before the time of trouble, it was the same thing: The owl screeched, and the samovar hissed, it never stopped.

GAEV: What time of trouble?

FIRS: Why, before the emancipation of the serfs.

Pause.

LYUBOV ANDREEVNA: Let's go, dear friends, shall we, it's getting dark. *(To ANYA.)* You've got tears in your eyes . . . What is it, my pet? *(Embraces her.)*

ANYA: I'm fine, Mama. It's nothing.

TROFIMOV: Someone's coming.

A PASSERBY appears in a shabby, white cap and a coat; he is slightly drunk.

PASSERBY: Permit me to inquire, may I pass through here to get to the train station?

GAEV: You may. Go down that road.

PASSERBY: I'm deeply grateful. *(Coughs.)* What superb weather we're having . . . *(Recites.)* "My brother, my suffering brother . . . Come down to the Volga, whose moan . . . " *(To VARYA.)* Mademoiselle, please, give a poor starving Russian thirty kopeks . . .

VARYA cries out in fear.

LOPAKHIN: *(Angrily.)* This has gone too far!

LYUBOV ANDREEVNA: *(Stunned.)* Here . . . take this . . . *(Searches in her purse.)* I have no silver . . . Never mind, here's a gold piece . . .

PASSERBY: I'm deeply grateful! *(Exits.)*

Laughter.

VARYA: *(Frightened.)* I'm leaving . . . I'm leaving . . . Oh, Mamochka, the servants at home have nothing to eat, and you gave him a gold piece.

LYUBOV ANDREEVNA: What are you going to do with me, I'm such a silly fool! I'll give you everything I have. Yermolai Alekseich, please, lend me some more money! . . .

LOPAKHIN: Yes, madam.

LYUBOV ANDREEVNA: Come, ladies and gentlemen, time to go. Oh, yes, Varya, we've just made a match for you. Congratulations.

VARYA: *(In tears.)* Mama, you musn't joke about that.

LOPAKHIN: "Oh-phel-i-a, get thee to a nunnery . . . "

GAEV: It's been so long since I've played a game of billiards, my hands are shaking.

LOPAKHIN: "Oh-phel-i-a, o nymph, remember me in thy prayers!"

LYUBOV ANDREEVNA: Come, ladies and gentlemen. It's almost suppertime.

VARYA: How he frightened me. My heart is pounding.

LOPAKHIN: May I remind you, ladies and gentlemen: On the twenty-second of August, the cherry orchard will be sold. Think about it! Think! . . .

They all leave, except TROFIMOV and ANYA.

ANYA: *(Laughing.)* The stranger frightened Varya off, thank goodness, now we're alone.

TROFIMOV: Varya's afraid we'll fall madly in love, she hasn't let us out of her sight for days. She's so narrow-minded, she can't understand we're above love. To overcome all obstacles, real and imagined, which stand in the path of freedom and happiness — that is our quest in life. Onward! We set forth, undaunted, toward that star, burning bright in the distance! Onward! Don't fall behind, my friends!

ANYA: *(Clasps her hands.)* How beautifully you talk!

Pause.

It's glorious here today!

TROFIMOV: Yes, the weather is amazing.

ANYA: What have you done to me, Petya, why don't I love the cherry orchard, as I did, once? I loved it so tenderly, I couldn't imagine any other place on earth more lovely than our orchard.

TROFIMOV: All Russia is our orchard. The land is vast and beautiful, there are many marvelous places in it.

Pause.

Just think, Anya: Your grandfather, your great-grandfather, and his forefathers before him, all were serf-owners, they all owned living souls, so isn't it possible, then, that in every blossom, every leaf, every tree trunk in the orchard, a human soul now gazes down upon us, can't you hear their voices . . . To own human souls — can't you see how this has transformed each and every one of us, those who have lived before and those who live today, so that you, your mother, your uncle, all of you, are no longer aware that you are alive at the expense of others, at the expense of those whom you would not even permit beyond your front hall . . . We have fallen behind, by two hundred years or so, at least, we have nothing left, absolutely nothing, no clear understanding of the past, we only philosophize, complain about our boredom, or drink vodka. And it's all so clear, can't you see, that to begin a new life, to live in the present, we must first redeem our past, put an end to it, and redeem it we shall, but only with suffering, only with extraordinary, everlasting toil and suffering. You must understand this, Anya.

ANYA: The house, in which we live, is no longer our house, and I shall leave it, I give you my word.

TROFIMOV: If you have the key, throw it in the well and run, run far, far away. Be free, like the wind.

ANYA: *(Ecstatic.)* How wonderfully you say it!

TROFIMOV: Believe me, Anya, believe me! I'm not even thirty yet, I'm young, I'm still a student, and yet, I've endured so much! Come winter, I'm hungry, sick, anxiety-ridden, poverty-stricken, like a beggar, and wherever fate carries me, there I shall be! And yet, all the while, every waking moment, day and night, my soul is filled with an indescribable premonition, a vision. A vision of happiness, Anya, I can see it now . . .

ANYA: *(Pensively.)* The moon is rising.

YEPIKHODOV is heard playing the guitar, the same melancholy song as before. The moon is rising. Somewhere near the poplars, VARYA is looking for ANYA and calling: "Anya! Where are you?"

TROFIMOV: Yes, the moon is rising.

Pause.

Here comes happiness, here it comes, closer and closer, I can already hear its footsteps. And if we don't see it, if we don't recognize it, then what does it matter? Others will!

VARYA'S voice: "Anya! Where are you?"

Varya, again! *(Angrily.)* It's disgraceful!

ANYA: I know! Let's go down to the river. It's lovely there.

TROFIMOV: Let's go.

They go.

VARYA's voice: "Anya! Anya!"

CURTAIN

from On the Harmful Effects of Tobacco
A Monologue in One Act

CHARACTER

Ivan Ivanovich Nyukhin

[In this tragicomedic monologue (Chekhov's favorite work), a brow-beaten schoolteacher, forced to give a lecture by his headmistress (who also happens to be his wife), breaks free from his bondage momentarily to dream of escape from his miserable existence.]

IVAN IVANOVICH NYUKHIN, his wife's husband, she being the proprietress of a music conservatory and boarding school for young ladies. The scene takes place on the dais of an auditorium in a provincial club.

Enter NYUKHIN, wearing long side-whiskers, with no moustache, and an old, threadbare tailcoat. He strides in majestically, bows, and adjusts his waistcoat.

NYUKHIN: Ladies, and, in a manner of speaking, gentlemen. *(Combs his whiskers.)* It has been suggested to my wife that I deliver a public lecture here today for charitable purposes. Well, why not? If I'm supposed to lecture, I'll lecture. It's all the same to me, really. I mean, I'm not a professor, well of course I'm not, in fact, I have no academic degree of any kind, but, nevertheless, and be that as it may, I have worked these past thirty years, worked without cease, I might very well add, to the detriment of my own health and so on and so forth, worked on issues of purest science, reflecting upon them, even writing scholarly articles on them from time to time, if you can imagine, well not exactly scholarly, but, if you'll pardon the expression, sort of scholarly, so to speak. Incidentally, I wrote a very extensive article recently, entitled: "Certain insects and their adverse effects." My daughters liked it very much, particularly the part about the bedbugs, but then I reread it and tore it to pieces. Because it's all the same in the end, really, you know, whether you write articles or not, you just can't get by without insect powder. We've even got bedbugs in the piano . . . I have chosen, as it were, for the topic of today's lecture: the harmful effects of tobacco on humans. Now I myself am a smoker, but my wife has instructed me to talk about the harmfulness of tobacco today, and so, as they say, that's that. If it's tobacco, then it's tobacco—really, I couldn't care less, but I do ask you, distinguished ladies and gentlemen, to try to take my lecture today as seriously as you possibly can, or else I shall suffer the consequences. And whosoever is put off by pure scientific discourse, then by all means, he or she is absolutely free to leave. *(Adjusts his waistcoat.)* I would, however, specifically like to call to attention any doctors who might be present, who might glean from my lecture some particularly useful information, inasmuch as tobacco, apart from its harmful effects, also has practical medical application. For example, if we were to place a fly into a snuffbox, then it would most likely die from a nervous disorder. Tobacco is considered, for the most part, to be a plant . . . When I give a lecture, I find that my right eye tends to twitch, so please, pay no attention to it, it's because I'm nervous. I'm a very nervous person, generally speaking, and my eye started twitching on the thirteenth of September, 1889, the very same day upon which my wife gave birth, so to speak, to our fourth daughter, Varvara. All my daughters were born on the thirteenth day of the month. However *(Looks at his watch.)* in view of the shortage of time, let us not stray from the subject of our lecture. At this time I should call to your attention that my wife runs both a music conservatory and a private boarding school, well, not exactly a boarding school, but something along those lines. Confidentially, my wife is fond of complaining about financial difficulties, but she's got money stashed away, forty or fifty thousand rubles, to be exact, while I haven't got a kopek to my name, not one single kopek — oh well, what's the use in talking about it! I manage the housekeeping department in the boarding school. I buy the supplies, supervise the servants, keep the accounts, stitch the copy books, get rid of the bedbugs, walk my wife's dog, catch the mice . . . Last evening, it was my responsibility to provide the cook with flour and oil, because we were having blinis. Well, today, to make a long story short, after the blinis were already made, my wife came into the kitchen to inform us that three of the pupils would not be eating blinis, because they had swollen glands. And, so it seems, we found ourselves with an overabundance of blinis. What were we supposed to do with them? At first, my wife ordered me to store them in the cellar, but she thought for a moment, and then she said: "Oh, go eat them yourself, dummy." That's what she calls me when she's in a bad mood: dummy. Or viper. Or Satan. Where did she get "Satan" from? She's always in a bad mood. Anyway, what happened was, I swallowed them whole, the blinis, swallowed them without chewing them, even, I was so hungry. I'm always hungry. Yesterday, for example, she wouldn't give me any dinner. "What's the point in feeding you, dummy?" However *(Glances at his watch.)* we're digressing again, we're off the subject. As I was saying . . . You'd much rather be listening to a love song right now, wouldn't you, or a symphony, or an aria . . . *(Bursts into song.)* "We will never blink an eye, when we hear the battle cry!" I never can remember where that comes from . . . By the way, I forgot to tell you that, in my wife's music conservatory, in addition to managing the housekeeping, I also have the responsibility of teaching mathematics, physics, chemistry, geography, history, musical theory, literature, etcetera etcetera. For dancing, singing, and drawing lessons my wife charges extra, although I am the dancing and singing instructor as well. Our music conservatory is located on Five Dogs Lane, Number 13. That's why I've been so unlucky in life, in all likelihood, because we live at House Number 13. And my daughters were all born on the thirteenth day of the month, and our house has thirteen windows . . . Oh, what's the use of talking about it! My wife is available by appointment, at our home, any time of day, and brochures can be obtained, if you wish, from the porter at the door, thirty kopeks a copy. *(Takes some brochures from his pocket.)* I happen to have a supply on me for distribution, if anyone's interested. Thirty kopeks each! Anyone want one? *(Pause.)* No one? How about twenty kopeks! *(Pause.)* Too bad. That's right, house number thirteen! Nothing has worked out for me in life, I've gotten older, and duller . . . Here I am, delivering a lecture to you, with a great big smile on my face, but deep down inside I want to scream at the top of my lungs, I want to fly away to the ends of the earth. I want to weep . . . and I've no one to tell my troubles to . . . What about my daughters, you say . . . Well, what about them? When I try to talk to them, they only laugh in my face . . . My wife has seven daughters . . . No, sorry, six . . . *(Quickly.)* Seven! The eldest one, Anna, is twenty-seven, and the youngest is seventeen. Ladies and gentlemen! *(Glances around.)* I'm so unhappy, I've become a fool, a nobody, and yet, really and truly, you see standing before you the most fortunate of fathers. Really and truly. And that's as it should be, what more can I say. If only you knew! I've been married to my wife for thirty-three years, and I can safely say that these have been the best years of my life, well, maybe not exactly the best, but something along those lines. They have flown by, in a word, like one happy moment, so to speak, and curse them all, curse them. *(Glances around.)* Anyway, she still hasn't arrived, she's not here yet, so I can say whatever I like . . . I'm terribly frightened . . . I'm frightened whenever she looks at me. What was I saying? Oh yes: My daughters are taking a long time getting themselves married, probably because they're shy, and also because they never get to meet any men. My wife doesn't like giving parties, she never invites anyone over for dinner, she's such a miserable, miserly, hellish sort of woman, and so no one ever comes to visit us, but . . . I'll let you in on a secret . . . *(Comes down to the footlights.)* My daughters can be found on all major holidays at their aunt's, Natalya Semyonovna's, you know, the one who suffers from rheumatism and goes around wearing this horrendous yellow dress with the black spots that looks like it has cockroaches crawling all over it. Go and visit, they'll even feed you. And if my wife isn't there, you might even . . . you know . . . *(Makes a gesture of drinking.)* I should tell you, by the way, it only takes one glass and away I go, and oh, do I I feel good inside, so good, and at the same time so sad, I can't tell you how sad I feel then, I start thinking of when I was young, and then suddenly for some reason I feel like running away, oh, if only you knew how much I wanted to run away! *(Passionately.)* To run, to throw everything to the winds and just run, without once looking back . . . and where? It doesn't matter where . . . if only to run from this vulgar, rotten, worthless, good-for-nothing life, which has made an old man of me, a pitiful, pathetic old fool, a wretched old idiot, to run from this stupid, petty, shallow, miserable, miserable, miserable miser, to run from my wife, who has tortured me for thirty-three years, to run from the conservatory, from the kitchen, from my wife's money, from all the stupidity and vulgarity . . . and stop somewhere far far away, out in a field somewhere, and stand there like a tree, or a telegraph pole, or a scarecrow, under the wide-open sky, and gaze all night at the silent moon shining above, and forget, forget . . . Oh, how I wish never again to remember, never! . . . How I long to tear off this wretched old coat, the coat I was married in thirty-three years ago . . . *(Tears off coat.)* the coat in which I give my never-ending lectures for charitable purposes . . . Take that! *(Throws coat on ground and tramples on it.)* And that! I'm old, and poor, and pathetic, like this shabby old waistcoat with its threadbare seams . . . *(Indicates the back.)* I don't want anything! I'm above all this! Once upon a time I was young, and brilliant, I went to the university, I had dreams, I was a human being . . . And now, now I want nothing! Nothing, only leave me in peace . . . leave me in peace! *(Glances around, puts on his coat.)* There's my wife, she's waiting out there in the wings . . . She's come at last, and she's waiting for me . . . *(Looks at his watch.)* We're out of time . . . If she asks you, then please, I beg of you, tell her that the lecture did take place . . . that the dummy—that is to say, me, that I conducted myself with complete decorum. *(Looks around, clears his throat.)* She's looking this way . . . *(Raises his voice.)* And thus, in conclusion, based on the evidence presented here today, as I have proven, that tobacco is a terribly poisonous substance, it therefore follows that you should not smoke under any circumstances, and I venture to say, furthermore, that I hope that my lecture "On the Harmful Effects of Tobacco" has been of benefit to you, to whatever extent. There. I've said it. And now I feel much better. *"Dixi et animam levavi!"* *(Bows and exits majestically.)*

CURTAIN

Chekhov

THE READING ROOM

YOUNG ACTORS AND THEIR TEACHERS

Bartlett, Rosamund. *Chekhov: Scenes from a Life*. London: Free Press, 2004.

Bruford, W. H. *Chekhov and His Russia*. Hamden, Conn.: Archon Books, 1971.

Hahn, Beverly. *Chekhov: A Study of the Major Stories and Plays*. Cambridge: Cambridge University Press, 1977.

Hingley, Ronald. "Chekhov's Russia." *Anton Chekhov's Plays*. Eugene K. Bristow, ed. New York: Norton, 1977.

Mirsky, D. S. *A History of Russian Literature*. New York: Knopf, 1958.

Pritchett, V. S. *A Spirit Set Free*. New York: Vintage, 1988.

Rayfield, Donald. *Anton Chekhov: A Life*. Evanston, Ill.: Northwestern University Press, 2000.

Valency, Maurice. *The Breaking String: The Plays of Anton Chekhov*. New York: Oxford University Press, 1966.

SCHOLARS, STUDENTS, PROFESSORS

Benedetti, Jean, tr. and ed. *The Moscow Art Theater Letters*. New York: Routledge, 1991.

_____. *"Dear Writer. . . Dear Actress . . .": The Love Letters of Olga Knipper and Anton Chekhov*. London: Methuen, 1996.

Bunin, I. A. *Vospominania*. Paris: Vozrozhdenie, l950.

Callow, Philip. *Chekhov, the Hidden Ground: A Biography*. London: Constable, 1998.

This extensive bibliography lists books about the playwright according to whom the books might be of interest. Also listed are editions of the playwright's works used for this book. Sources Cited in This Book lists the sources from which the author has quoted. If you would like to research further something that interested you in the text, you can find the references in this section.

Chudakov, A. P. *Chekhov's Poetics*. Edwina Cruise and Donald Dragt, trs. Ann Arbor, Mich.: Ardis, 1983.

Eekman, Thomas, ed. *Critical Essays on Anton Chekhov*. Boston: G. K. Hall, 1989.

Gilles, Daniel. *Chekhov: Observer without Illusion*. New York: Funk & Wagnalls, 1968.

Gottlieb, Vera, and Paul Allain, eds. *The Cambridge Companion to Chekhov*. New York: Cambridge University Press, 2000.

Jackson, Robert Louis, ed. *Chekhov: A Collection of Critical Essays*. Englewood Cliffs, N.J.: Prentice-Hall, 1976.

Kirk, Irina. *Anton Chekhov*. Boston: Twayne, 1976.

Kuprin, A. I. *Sobranie sochineny v devyati tomax. Tom II*. Moscow: Izdatelstvo "Khudozhestvannaya Literatura," 1973.

Rayfield, Donald. *Chekhov: The Evolution of His Art*. New York: Barnes and Noble, 1975.

Stanislavsky, Konstantin. *My Life in Art*. J. J. Robbins, ed. London: Methuen, 1989.

Stein, Peter. *Mon Tchekhov*. Arles: Actes sud, 2002.

Tulloch, John. *Chekhov: A Structuralist Study*. New York: Harper and Row, 1980.

Welleck, Rene, and Nonna D. Welleck, eds. *Chekhov: New Perspectives*. Englewood Cliffs, N.J.: Prentice-Hall, 1984.

Williames, Lee J. *Anton Chekhov: The Iconoclast*. Scranton, Pa.: University of Scranton Press, 1989.

THEATERS, PRODUCERS

McConkey, James, ed. *Chekhov and Our Age*. Ithaca, N.Y.: Cornell University Press, n.d.

Simmons, Ernest J. *Chekhov: A Biography*. Boston: Little, Brown, 1962.

Turkov, Andrei, ed. *Anton Chekhov and His Times*. Fayetteville: University of Arkansas Press, 1995.

ACTORS, DIRECTORS, PROFESSIONALS

Clyman, Toby W., ed. *A Chekhov Companion*. Westport, Conn.: Greenwood Press, 1985.

Gilman, Richard. *Chekhov's Plays: An Opening into Eternity.* New Haven, Conn.: Yale University Press, 1995.

Gottlieb, Vera. *Chekhov and the Vaudeville.* Cambridge: Cambridge University Press, 1982.

Heim, Michael, and Simon Karlinsky. *Anton Chekhov's Life and Thought: Selected Letters and Commentary.* Berkeley: University of California Press, 1973.

Hingley, Ronald. *A New Life of Anton Chekhov.* New York: Knopf, 1976.

Lucas, F. L. *The Drama of Chekhov, Synge, Yeats, and Pirandello.* London: Cassell, 1963.

Magarshack, David. *Chekhov the Dramatist.* London: John Lehmann, Ltd., 1952.

_____. *Chekhov: A Life.* New York: Grove Press, 1952.

_____. *The Real Chekhov.* London: George Allen & Unwin, Ltd., 1972.

Miles, Patrick, tr. and ed. *Chekhov on the British Stage.* Cambridge: Cambridge University Press, 1993.

Nemirovich-Danchenko. *My Life in the Russian Theater.* John Cournos, tr. London: Geoffrey Bles, 1968.

Pitcher, Harvey. *Chekhov's Leading Lady.* London: John Murray, Ltd., 1979.

Rocamora, Carol. "I take your hand in mine . . . ," an original play based on the correspondence between Chekhov and Olga Knipper. Lyme, N.H.: Smith and Kraus, 2000.

Troyat, Henri. *Chekhov.* New York: Fawcett Colombine, 1986.

Winner, Thomas. *Chekhov and His Prose.* New York: Holt, Rinehart and Winston, 1966.

Worrall, Nick. *File on Chekhov.* London: Methuen, 1986.

THE EDITIONS OF CHEKHOV'S WORKS USED FOR THIS BOOK

Chekhov, Anton. *The Early Plays.* Carol Rocamora, tr. Lyme, N.H.: Smith and Kraus, 1996.

_____. *Four Plays.* Carol Rocamora, tr. Lyme, N.H.: Smith and Kraus, 1996.

_____. *The Vaudevilles and Other Short Works.* Carol Rocamora, tr. Lyme, N.H.: Smith and Kraus, 1996.

SOURCES CITED IN THIS BOOK

The paraphrased quote on page 37 is found in: Gilles, Daniel. *Chekhov: Observer without Illusion*. New York: Funk & Wagnalls, 1968.

All letters of Chekhov quoted in this book have been translated by Carol Rocamora directly from the original Russian. See Chekhov, Anton Pavlovich. *Polnoe sobranie schineniy i psem v tridtsati tomax*. Moskva: Izdatelstvo 'Nauka,' 1974–82 (translation: *Chekhov: The Complete Collected Works and Letters in 30 Volumes*. Moscow, 1974).

The letter to Tikhonov dated February 22, 1892, on page 11, was translated by Carol Rocamora. The translation has not yet been published.

For general collections of Chekhov's letters, see: Benedetti, Jean, tr. and ed. *The Moscow Art Theater Letters*. New York: Routledge, 1991; Heim, Michael, and Simon Karlinsky. *Anton Chekhov's Life and Thought: Selected Letters and Commentary*. Berkeley: University of California Press, 1973.

INDEX

The entries in the index above include highlights from the main In an Hour essay portion of the book.

About the Author

Dr. Carol Rocamora is a professor, playwright, translator, and critic. Her three volumes of Chekhov's complete translated dramatic works have been published by Smith and Kraus. She teaches at New York University's Tisch School of the Arts, where she has been the recipient of the David Payne Carter Award for Teaching in Excellence. She also teaches at Columbia University in the MFA Theatre Arts Program and guest-lectures at the Juilliard School and the Yale School of Drama. She was the founder and artistic director of the Philadelphia Festival Plays at Annenberg Center. She has written about theater for *The Nation* and the *New York Times* and currently contributes to *The Guardian* and *American Theatre*. She has completed *Rubles*, a collection of original plays inspired by Chekhov's short stories, and is currently working on a biography of Chekhov.

We thank Carol Rocamora and her agent Susan Smith, MBA Literary Agents Ltd., whose enlightened permissions policies reflects an understanding that copyright law is intended to both protect the rights of creators of intellectual property as well as to encourage its use for the public good.

Know the playwright, love the play.

Open a new door to theater study, performance, and audience satisfaction with these Playwrights In an Hour titles.

ANCIENT GREEK

Aeschylus   Aristophanes   Euripides   Sophocles

RENAISSANCE

William Shakespeare

MODERN

Anton Chekhov   Noël Coward   Lorraine Hansberry
Henrik Ibsen   Arthur Miller   Molière   Eugene O'Neill
Arthur Schnitzler   George Bernard Shaw   August Strindberg
Frank Wedekind   Oscar Wilde   Thornton Wilder
Tennessee Williams

CONTEMPORARY

Edward Albee   Alan Ayckbourn   Samuel Beckett
Theresa Rebeck   Sarah Ruhl   Sam Shepard   Tom Stoppard
August Wilson

To purchase or for more information
visit our web site inanhourbooks.com